Andrea Caffi

The New York Essays

Andrea Caffi

The New York Essays

Edited and Introduced by: Mike Tyldesley

Afterword by: Alberto Castelli

little big eye publishing

Andrea Caffi: The New York Essays © 2026 by Mike Tyldesley and Alberto Castelli is licensed under Creative Commons Attribution-NonCommercial 4.0 International ⓒⓒ ⓘ Ⓢ. To view a copy of this license, visit www.creativecommons.org/licenses/by-nc/4.0/.

Library of Congress Control Number: 2026932765

ISBN: 978-1-960821-04-1

Cover Design by: Mykell Gates Jamil

Image Credit: 'Andrea Caffi', anonymous photograph, unknown. Source: *Nonluoghi*, https://www.nonluoghi.info/old/fofi.html

Published by little big eye publishing, Charlotte, NC, 28205, USA, www.littlebigeyepublishing.com/.

Table of Contents

Introduction

Andrea Caffi was living in Toulouse in September 1945 when the first of the articles in this collection was written.[1] He arrived there after having fled Paris in June 1940 as part of a group with Nicola Chiaromonte, Mario Levi, and the future historian of Russian Populism, Franco Venturi.[2] They fled Paris as Hitler's army entered it. Chiaromonte left Toulouse and Caffi behind in March 1941. He went to New York via Algeria (where he met Albert Camus). This proved crucial for the genesis of the essays in this book. Caffi and Chiaromonte — the two had met in May 1932 in Paris, having been introduced to each other by the novelist Alberto Moravia[3] — were only to get back in touch at the start of 1945, with a letter from Chiaromonte in New York dated the 16th January 1945.[4]

By 1945 Caffi was 58. Born in St. Petersburg in 1887, he had lived a nomadic life. He'd frequently been in trouble with the authorities and their respective secret police forces — the Okhrana in Imperial Russia, the Cheka in Revolutionary Russia, the OVRA in Fascist Italy, and finally the Gestapo and Milice in Vichy France. From 1926 onwards he had settled in France, where he would die, in Paris, in 1955. This is not the place to tell the full story of his life. What we will do in this introduction is place him in relation to the journals in New York — a city which he never visited — that published his work between 1945 and 1948.[5]

---

1 The second was actually written in August 1945, but he was already living in Toulouse when that was written.

2 Nicola Chiaromonte (1905–1972), Italian writer and activist. Mario Levi (1905–1973), Italian anti-fascist activist and brother of the writer Natalia Ginzburg. Franco Venturi (1914–1994), Italian historian.

3 Nicola Chiaromonte, "Introduction", in Andrea Caffi, *A Critique of Violence*, Indianapolis, Bobbs-Merrill, 1970, p. vii.

4 Mario Bresciani, (ed), *«Cosa Sperare?» Il carteggio tra Andrea Caffi e Nicola Chiaromonte: un dialogo sulla rivoluzione (1932–1955)*, Napoli, Edizioni Scientifiche Italiane, 2012, p. 148.

5 Some sources for Caffi's life: in English; Nicola Chiaromonte's introduction to A. Caffi, *A Critique of Violence*; Alberto Castelli, *The Peace Discourse in Europe*, London, Routledge, 2019, see Chapter 12, "Thinking outside politics"; Marco Bresciani, *Learning from History*, London, Verso, 2024, (a translation of his 2017 *Quale Antifascismo*. That book's subtitle was "History of Giustizia e Libertà") is useful on Caffi's role in *Giustizia e Libertà*, the Italian

So, how did this obscure Italian socialist living in a state of some penury[6] end up writing a fair number of articles for *avant-garde* publications in a city on the other side of the world? The explanation for the wider picture becomes clearer if we explain the specifics of the connection between Caffi and *politics*, the journal in New York where Caffi's work first appeared, and the most famous of these journals overall.

The story of Caffi's connection with *politics* possibly started some time in 1942. This is based on the statement by Lionel Abel that he first met Nicola Chiaromonte at the house of Dwight Macdonald[7] in the Winter of 1942,[8] around eighteen months after Chiaromonte had left Toulouse. Against this, Amanda Swain suggests that actually Chiaromonte met

---

anti-fascist movement associated with Carlo Rosselli; my own *Liberate and Federate*, Sparnäs, Irene Publishing, 2024; Natalia Ginzburg, *Family Lexicon*, London, Daunt Books, 2018, has some material on Caffi, there called 'Cafi'; Lionel Abel, *The Intellectual Follies*, New York, W W Norton and Co, 1984 has memories of Caffi in Paris in the 1950s. Marco Bresciani's "Socialism, Fascism and Anti-Totalitarianism", *History of European Ideas*, Vol. 40, No. 7, 2014, is a study of the intellectual relationship of Caffi and Chiaromonte. In Italian; Marco Bresciani, *La rivoluzione perduta, Andrea Caffi nell'Europa del Novecento*, Bologna, il Mulino, 2009, is a biography. In French, Clara Malraux, *Et pourtant j'étais libre,* Paris, Grasset, 1979, has wartime memories of Caffi from Toulouse. Finally, Chiaromonte's "Lost Italians", in his *The Worm of Consciousness*, New York, Harcourt Brace Jovanovitch, 1977, gives an insight into the life of Italian socialist exiles in Toulouse in the early 1940s.

6 At this distance in time it is hard to discuss such issues, but there may have been an element of choice in Caffi's circumstances. Chiaromonte talks of how efforts to provide him with ways out of his condition proved futile due to a "desire not to "fit in" in a society which he profoundly disliked." Chiaromonte, "Introduction", Caffi, *A Critique of Violence*, p. ix. Marion Labeÿ in an article mainly concentrating on Caffi's time in Russia immediately after the Bolshevik Revolution, offers some interesting insights into his personal life, including his homosexuality, citing his self-definition in a letter of January 1946 to Niccolò Tucci as an "étranger". Marion Labeÿ, "Andrea Caffi et la Révolution Bolchevique, Une crise personelle au «crepuscule de la civilization europeénne» (1917–1923)", *Cahiers Jaurès*, 2021, 1, no. 239–240, see pp. 86-88, letter to Tucci, p.86. Just to complicate matters, Chiaromonte also notes that Caffi was "a man of the most affable and amiable sort", p. viii.

7 Lionel Abel (1910–2001), American playwright, essayist, translator. Dwight Macdonald (1906–1982), American critic, writer and editor.

8 Lionel Abel, "Innocence and the Intellectual" (a "Reconsideration: Nicola Chiaromonte"), *The New Republic*, 24 March 1986, p. 38.

Macdonald in mid-1943, around the time of Macdonald's departure from *Partisan Review*.[9] Crucially, either way, this is before the first edition of *politics*, in February 1944. Given the resources at hand for both the prehistory and the history of *politics*, this is certainly not the place for a potted history of the journal's foundation or history. We can, however, say a few things of pertinence.[10] The journal, *politics*, was started by Dwight and Nancy Macdonald[11] after they 'split' from *Partisan Review*. Dwight Macdonald had been an editor and one of the key writers on *Partisan Review,* and Nancy Macdonald its managing editor. Dwight Macdonald had started to have political disagreements with the other editors — especially regarding the 'line' to be taken regarding the Second World War then raging — and also disagreed with the way the *Review* was moving away, in his view, from politics as a focus. So, they left in late 1943 with the intention of setting up a new journal.

They had around them some talented people. Kevin Coogan stresses the role in the endeavour of four women: Nancy Macdonald, Mary McCarthy, Hannah Arendt[12] (who never actually wrote for the journal), and Simone Weil.[13] There were also some important male members of the team, and one such was Chiaromonte. Sumner suggests that during "his years in New York in the 1940s, Chiaromonte became Macdonald's closest friend and adviser".[14] Indeed, it has been suggested that William

---

9 Amanda Swain, "Utopia in New York: Nicola Chiaromonte and the New York Intellectuals' "Superstition of Science"", *Modern Intellectual History*, 21 (2024), pp. 410-440, p. 426, see especially footnote 92, which goes into this issue in detail, with evidence suggesting her account is more likely than Abel's. Thanks to Dr. Swain for pointing this out.

10 A minimal starting point for these subjects would be: Michael Wreszin, *A Rebel in Defence of Tradition: The Life and politics of Dwight Macdonald*, New York, BasicBooks, 1994, and Gregory Sumner, *Dwight Macdonald and the politics Circle*, Ithaca, Cornell University Press, 1996.

11 Nancy Macdonald (1910-1996), managing editor and activist.

12 Mary McCarthy (1912-1989), American novelist, critic and activist. Hannah Arendt (1906-1975), German/American political theorist and historian.

13 Simone Weil (1909-1943), French philosopher. As Weil died in August 1943, her role at *politics* was posthumous. Coogan calls her "the most powerful intellectual influence on the journal". Kevin Coogan, "Introduction", Dwight Macdonald, *The Root is Man,* Brooklyn, Autonomedia, 1995, p. 22. Staughton Lynd, in an essay in a book on Weil, described her as the "patron saint" of the magazine, cited in Sumner, *Dwight Macdonald...*, p. 56.

14 Sumner, *Dwight Macdonald...*, p. 27.

Phillips's[15] (one of the *Partisan Review's* editors Macdonald left behind) barbed comment "Dwight is looking for a disciple who will tell him what to think" was aimed at Chiaromonte.[16]

Before moving on, it is worth registering the achievement of the journal. Although the circulation was never large — Coogan suggests it never had more than 5,000 subscribers[17], although this may give a false impression of reach, as Lewis Coser[18], one of the team, estimated that three people read each copy[19] — the list of writers that contributed to it was stellar. An edited version of a list given by Coogan would include: Simone Weil, Albert Camus, Victor Serge, Georges Bataille, Jean-Paul Sartre, Simone de Beauvoir, Mary McCarthy, Paul Goodman, Marshall McLuhan, Irving Howe and C. Wright Mills.[20] One might also add George Orwell to that list and there were others: for instance, Anton Pannekoek, a target of Lenin's 1920 work, *"Left-Wing" Communism, an Infantile Disorder.*

Chiaromonte had a role in addition to the input of his political viewpoint: talent scout[21], and in that role he introduced a number of writers to the journal. Sumner indicates that he was responsible for Niccolo Tucci[22] (later a writer on the *New Yorker* magazine) writing for *politics*, and that it was Chiaromonte who had championed Simone Weill during the Summer of 1945.[23] From our point of view, however, his most important introduction was, of course, his old friend Andrea Caffi.[24] So we might suggest that the reason Caffi's writing appeared in the three New York journals in the mid to late 1940s was ultimately because of the role of Nicola Chiaromonte in bringing him to the attention of the team at *politics*, and in particular to the attention of Dwight Macdonald.

---

15 William Phillips (1907–2002), American editor and writer.

16 Sumner, *Dwight Macdonald...*, p. 31.

17 Kevin Coogan, "Introduction", p. 22.

18 Lewis Coser (1913–2003), German/American sociologist.

19 Sumner, *Dwight Macdonald...*, p. 37.

20 Coogan, "Introduction", p. 22. A fairly full index appeared in the Winter 1948 edition, which was issue 39 of 42. Pages 64–66 are the authors. All editions of the journal can now be accessed at the Biblioteca Gino Bianco website: https://www.bibliotecaginobainco.it

21 Sumner, *Dwight Macdonald...*, p. 33.

22 Niccolo Tucci (1908–1999), European/American writer.

23 Sumner, *Dwight Macdonald...*, pp. 55–56.

24 Sumner, Op. Cit., p. 33.

Before moving on from *politics*, it is worth making a couple of points about Caffi's writing there. The first is that it was anonymous. All of his six articles for the magazine appeared under the pseudonym "European". Macdonald finally let the cat out of the bag in the book version of his *The Root is Man* when he introduced a piece by Caffi (see below) as follows: "It is by Andrea Caffi, a historian and philosopher who used to write for *politics* under the pseudonym "European".[25]

The second is to signal the extent to which Caffi's articles represented a contribution to debates and discussions going on in the team that produced *politics*. The 1945 pieces, "The Automatization of European People" and "Towards a Socialist Program" were, rather than articles *per se*, actually 'made' into articles from material in letters that Caffi had sent from Toulouse to Chiaromonte and Macdonald. The 1946 contributions, "Is a Revolutionary War a Contradiction in Terms" and "Notes on Mass Culture" are both concerned to debate points made by Macdonald (in both) and Melvin J Lasky[26] ("Notes..."). It is only with the 1947 articles, "Violence and Sociability" and "The French Condition" that we find 'standalone' pieces that we can see as essays, rather than contributions to an on-going discussion.

With "The French Condition", published in the July-August 1947 edition, "European's" voice in *politics*, for whatever reason, goes silent. But this was not the end of Caffi as a voice in New York. He next featured in the sole edition of a journal called *possibilities*.

The single edition of this journal appeared dated "Winter 1947/8", with a copyright of 1947. This all suggests that the journal appeared in late

---

25 Dwight Macdonald, *The Root is Man*, Alhambra (CA), The Cunningham Press, 1953, p. 62.

26 Melvin J Lasky (1920–2004). Writer and editor, Lasky was involved closely with the journals *Der Monat* and *Encounter*, which he edited from 1958, remaining connected to the journal until its closure in 1991. These journals had received financial support from the CIA-funded Congress for Cultural Freedom, a fact revealed in 1967 by *Ramparts* magazine. A key source on this episode is Frances Stonor Saunders, *Who Paid the Piper? The CIA and the Cultural Cold War*, London, Granta, 2000. This is worth mentioning as other members of the *politics* team, including Macdonald and Chiaromonte were to greater or lesser degrees part of this 'world' in the 1950s and beyond.

1947. It was published by Wittenborn, Schultz, Inc of New York[27], and it was the fourth in a series called "Problems of Contemporary Art", complemented by a series of "Documents of Modern Art".[28] The editorial team of the journal was Robert Motherwell (art), Harold Rosenberg (writing), Pierre Chareau (architecture) and John Cage[29] (music).[30] The approach of the journal is indicated in the statement made by Motherwell and Rosenberg on its first page. It starts: "This is a magazine of artists and writers who "practice" in their work their own experience without seeking to transcend it in academic, group or political formulas." It presents politics as a choice that can be made, but one which precludes art: "Once the political choice has been made, art and literature ought of course to be given up." And the statement ends: "If one is to continue to paint or write as the political trap seems to close upon him he must have the extremest faith in sheer possibility. In his extremism he shows that he has recognised how drastic the political presence is."[31] Clearly, *possibilities* was a different type of magazine to *politics*. Despite that, as well as Caffi, another two authors from *politics*, Lionel Abel and Paul Goodman[32], were among the writers featured in it. (In both cases, they published pieces of creative writing there.)

In her study, *Issues in Abstract Expressionism: The Artist Run Periodicals*, Ann Eden Gibson, in a short presentation of *possibilities*, makes a number of points clear. The approach of the journal was very much that implied by Motherwell and Rosenberg (she identifies them as the people who really ran the journal, regardless of the full list of editors)[33]

---

27 George Wittenborn (1905-1974), a German emigré in the USA, ran a series of businesses: bookshop, publishers, art gallery. With Heinz Schultz (1904-1954) from 1939, he ran an art book shop and publishers.

28 See the back cover of *possibilities* for details of both series.

29 Robert Motherwell (1915-1991), American painter. Harold Rosenberg (1906-1978), American art critic and writer. Pierre Chareau (1883-1950), French architect and designer. John Cage (1912-1992), American composer and music theorist.

30 Descriptions as: *possibilities*, p. 1.

31 *Ibid*, all quotes in this paragraph.

32 Paul Goodman (1911-1972), American writer and public intellectual.

33 Ann Eden Gibson, *Issues in Abstract Expressionism: The Artist Run Periodicals*, Ann Arbor, UMI Research Press, 1990. Her chapter on *possibilities* is pp. 33-39, and the comment on Motherwell and Rosenberg is p. 33 It is worth noting that in producing her book, which also deals with

in their 'manifesto'. Much of her initial discussion is devoted to the impact on the journal of Motherwell's commitment to an antistructural Dada collage influenced methodology. She quotes him to the effect that the purpose of the journal was not 'theoretical'. Rather, in Motherwell's words: "very factual descriptions presenting the thing — without theory."[34] This was partly why — as Gibson shows — a contemporary commentator on the journal, Parker Tyler, called its *avant-garde* status into question.[35]

Gibson does not mention Caffi's article *On Mythology* or venture any reason why it appeared in the journal. The translation was by Lionel Abel, who also had a play published in the journal: it is possible that he was involved in its appearance.[36] That said, she includes a transcript of it in the collection of material from *possibilities* in her book (each journal examined has such a section, including written and visual material). It remains, therefore, unclear quite why the piece appeared there, although it is not out of place. Perhaps the only other point of interest in the journal is that at the end of Caffi's piece is a picture of a poster in a Greek restaurant in New York (the Acropolis) and a brief note about the reaction to it of Carlo Levi[37] who had been having lunch there with "H.R." (presumably Harold Rosenberg).[38] Levi had known Caffi, for a time both activists in the *Giustizia e Libertà* anti-fascist movement, in Paris in the 1930s.[39]

The third New York journal that published Caffi was *Instead*. This was a considerable contrast stylistically from *possibilities*. That was a substantial, professionally published journal of 112 pages. *Instead* was a single sheet measuring approximately 18 inches by 24 inches (Arch C, or

---

Instead — see below — as well as other journals, Professor Gibson interviewed a number of the key figures. In respect of *possibilities,* she mentions Robert Motherwell. For our purposes given his role on both *politics* and *Instead,* the fact she singles out Lionel Abel for thanks in her acknowledgements for his assistance in her chapter on *Instead* is to be noted.

34 Gibson, Op. Cit., p. 34.

35 Gibson, Op. Cit., p. 33.

36 A point made by Jed Rasula, who discusses "On Mythology", mentioning Abel, in his *Acrobatic Modernism* from the Avant-Garde to Prehistory, Oxford, Oxford University Press, 2020, p. 376, see footnote 60.

37 Carlo Levi (1902–1975), Italian painter and writer.

38 *Possibilities*, no. 1, p. 95.

39 See M. Bresciani, *La rivoluzione perduta*, p. 212.

informally '4:3 poster size'). This was folded to give 16 "pages" which were used in a 'creative' way.[40] The unusual size and shape of *Instead* caused, according to Gibson, problems. She ventures that it being a single sheet perhaps led to some readers believing it to be a transient handout (although it had a cover price, some copies were given away) and not to be preserved.[41] She also quotes Lionel Abel to the effect that Roberto Matta[42], artist and leading figure in the magazine, actually designed it to be hard to follow articles 'around' the magazine making it a sort of labyrinth. Matta, in Abel's view, felt that if readers didn't know how to make their way through the magazine, then they weren't intelligent enough to read it.[43] In his own memoirs, Abel suggests that the formatting lost the journal readers, but notes that when tastes shifted in the 1960s the format appealed to those who saw old copies, and felt that when he was writing (1984) a journal with that format would find a public.[44]

No such issues attached to any of Caffi's four articles in the journal, which are fairly straightforwardly set out. Before moving off issues of this nature, we might note that some editions of the journal did not have a masthead, some were undated and some were unnumbered. This sometimes makes it hard to work out precisely which edition one needs to find to access an article. Gibson notes that issues 2 to 5/6 (a 'double' issue) were all published in 1948, and — evidently — numbered. There was an initial issue which had a 'rose' like form on the 'cover', which she designates as number 1 and one that has on its 'cover' a drawing of Georges Bataille by Alberto Giacometti which she designates as number 7 (this was probably published early in 1949: Gibson notes that Abel was paid by Patricia Connoly, Roberto Matta's wife prior to divorce in 1948, to work on the journal and that this included assembling the final issue after his move to Paris in December 1948[45]). One of Caffi's articles is in "1" and two are in

---

40 Given these points, Gibson's description — *Issues*, p. 41 — of *Instead* as being published in tabloid form may give readers a rather misleading view.

41 Gibson, Op. Cit., p. 41.

42 Roberto Matta Echaurren, usually known as Roberto Matta (1911–2002), Chilean artist, usually connected to the abstract expressionist and surrealist movements, although expelled from the latter by André Breton due to the circumstances of the suicide of Arshile Gorky.

43 Gibson, Op. Cit., p. 42.

44 Lionel Abel, *The Intellectual Follies*, p. 108.

45 Gibson, *Issues*, p. 73, footnote 1. Note that Connoly was also named — p. 41 — by Gibson as the person who financed the journal.

"7". As a result of this set of idiosyncrasies[46], it is extremely hard to be certain which editions are available in library collections. It appears that the New York Museum of Modern Art Library has the best extant collection.

Both Matta and Abel had connections to the surrealist movement. Matta had been inspired by Breton[47] and Abel had been chosen to edit *VVV* by Breton.[48] That said, *Instead* published material on a much wider range of topics than simply surrealism or art. It had a very marked tendency to publish European, especially French, philosophical writers, and one could argue that its 'roster', especially given its relatively short life, could compare to that of *politics*. As well as Abel, Matta and Caffi, the likes of Antonin Artaud, Breton himself, Maurice Blanchot, Emmanuel Levinas, Jean Wahl, Alexandre Kojève, and Martin Heidegger featured in its pages. In this, it arguably reflected the interests of Matta and perhaps especially Abel, who, as Gibson notes, had had conversations in 1943 and 1944 that resulted in the emergence of the journal. As such, Caffi's place in the journal is not a surprise (and indeed neither is that of Chiaromonte, who as well as being co-author of Caffi's "The Myth and Politics", contributed "A Note on the Movies" to issue 4.) Gibson, with her focus on issues in the art world, summarises the role of the journal as follows: "magazines like *Instead* provided a valuable source of information about the development of French Existentialism"[49] for American artists in the late forties. Her brief chapter on the journal[50] and the readings from the journal she reproduces[51] well bear out this judgement. That said, Gibson notes that if for Abel Existential ideas represented the focus of the journal, for Matta that wasn't the case: for Matta "*Instead* was, precisely just … *Instead*. Not Surrealism nor Existentialism."[52]

Caffi published four articles in the journal, with the first, "A Glance at Marx's Horizons", appearing in the first issue alongside pieces by

---

46 One might note as well Abel's comment regarding its production methods: "And so it must be realized that it [*Instead*] was not made up by people who were entirely sober." Op. Cit., p. 108.

47 André Breton (1896–1966), French surrealist writer and poet.

48 Gibson, *Issues*, pp. 41–42.

49 Gibson, Op. Cit., p. 46.

50 Gibson, Op. Cit., pp. 41–47.

51 Gibson, Op. Cit., pp. 265–304.

52 Gibson, Op. Cit., p. 42.

Antonin Artaud, André Breton (on Arshile Gorky), Niccolo Tucci, Lionel Abel, a translation from Alexandre Kojève, and "The Myth of Oedipus" adapted from the Greek by Meyer Schapiro. Caffi was there until the end, with "In Today's Newspapers" and "The Myth and Politics" appearing in the final issue.

The fourth location of Caffi's writing reproduced in this volume stretches our 'New York' theme. This is Dwight Macdonald's already mentioned book *The Root is Man.* This book, published in California in 1953, contains two major articles by Macdonald that had been published in *politics.* ("The Root is Man" and "The Responsibility of Peoples".) It also contains a sequence of footnotes indicating points on which he had changed his view, along with three appendices discussing aspects of his changed viewpoint ("B" starts with the heading "The main enemy is in Moscow"[53] and "C" starts: "I think the point at which I began to stop believing in pacifism as a political doctrine was the Russian blockade of Berlin."[54]) At the end of appendix "C" Macdonald introduces an "extraordinary manuscript submitted to me too late for inclusion in the last edition of *Politics.*"[55] This is Caffi's "Mass Politics and the Pax Americana". One might say that one of the few things on which Macdonald had not actually changed his mind was the quality of Caffi's work, such is the effusiveness with which he introduces the piece. We can justifiably include it here for two reasons. Firstly, Caffi thought he was submitting it to a New York magazine, and secondly, it has not, as far as we are aware, been reproduced since 1953 and accordingly even if it is stretching our definitions a little, it is right that this be once more made available to readers.

The piece derives from an article published by Caffi in an Italian journal, *Critica Sociale,* in November 1948 called "I Ragionamenti di Koestler".[56] This indicates that Caffi — who left Toulouse for Paris in early 1949 — probably wrote the piece while in Toulouse.[57] It is possible that this was the last piece Caffi ever wrote that was published in his lifetime. It is

---

53 Macdonald, *The Root is Man,* p. 58.
54 Macdonald, Op. Cit., p. 60. The blockade started in June 1948.
55 Macdonald, Op. Cit., p. 62.
56 See Bresciani, *La Rivoluzione perduta,* p. 287, footnote 135. The title means "Koestler's Reasoning".
57 See *Liberate and Federate,* p. 127 for my reasoning here.

certainly the last piece that was published in his lifetime in the English language.

Caffi moved to Paris, as already noted, in early 1949, and remained there until his death in 1955. He lived in the Hotel de l'Académie, on the rue des Saints-Pères in St Germain-des-Près, Paris. One of his neighbours for a while was American novelist Saul Bellow. Caffi may, indeed, have been the model for Mr Sammler in *Mr Sammler's Planet*.[58] While in Paris he worked as a 'reader' for the important French publisher Gallimard, and one of 'his' authors has left a generous tribute to his work there: Franco Venturi.[59] Caffi died on July 22nd, 1955. He was cremated and his ashes are in the Colombarium of the Père Lachaise cemetery.

We can finish with some brief points about the three people who made the New York essays of Andrea Caffi possible. Firstly, Dwight Macdonald is certainly not difficult to read about. We have already referenced a number of key works about him. The biography by Michael Wreszin and the study by Gregory Sumner are excellent starting points on him, and his interesting 'post-Caffi' career.

The second of the three is Lionel Abel. He has left an autobiography, already referenced in this chapter (*The Intellectual Follies*), which contains interesting material about Caffi from the time Abel knew him in Paris. He returned to Caffi, in 1970, when the collection of Caffi essays *A Critique of Violence* was published in English. He published an article in the journal *Commentary,* "What is Society? The Ideas of Andrea Caffi".[60] This is relatively easy to track down, but one point made near the start is worth highlighting. Abel, who was a professional translator *inter alia*, notes: "Complex things are said by Caffi again and again in his texts; but now the nuance, without which he thought one could hardly say them,

---

58 See Ch 8 of *Liberate and Federate*, "Sociable Hermit", for Caffi's life in Paris. I deal with the Mr Sammler question on p. 129.

59 This is, of course, the Franco Venturi who was in the party with Caffi that left Paris in 1940. See: Franco Venturi, *Roots of Revolution*, London, Phoenix Press, 2001. The reference to Caffi is in the 'Revised Author's Introduction' of 1972, p. xxxvii. In this context, Marco Bresciani's "Andrea Caffi's Intellectual Itinerary: A Long-Standing Loyalty to Herzen in the Twentieth Century", *Russica Romana*, XV, 2008, pp. 57-71, is extremely useful.

60 Lionel Abel, "What is Society? The Ideas of Andrea Caffi", *Commentary*, Vol. 50, No. 3, September 1970, pp. 45–55.

is gone. Reading over again, in *A Critique of Violence*, passages I first read in his own hand in letters to Nicola Chiaromonte, I was struck by the crudeness and heaviness of a prose which in the original, I must insist, was deft, light and often deadly. Poor Caffi!"[61] In some cases the essays in this volume are translated by Abel, and 'duplicate' (if only to some extent) the ones published in *A Critique of Violence*. The reader will, if they choose, be able to compare the translations. It is worth pointing out, though, that whereas Abel had the advantage of translating Caffi's original French, the translator of *A Critique of Violence* was working from an Italian translation of Caffi's French.

Finally, we should mention Nicola Chiaromonte. There is not, as yet, a biography of Chiaromonte in English. As with Caffi, there is a substantial literature in Italian about him, much of it recent. (As Amanda Swain has noted, there has been an "Italian rediscovery" of Chiaromonte in recent years.[62]) That said, in recent years there have been a number of interesting historical articles published about Chiaromonte. Marco Bresciani's important 2014 essay covering the relationship between Caffi and Chiaromonte has already been referred to here.[63] In 2017 Chiara Morbi and Paola Carlucci published a chapter about *Tempo Presente* in Giles Scott-Smith and Charlotte Lerg's edited volume *Campaigning Culture and the Global Cold War*.[64] *Tempo Presente* was a journal (ultimately CIA funded) that Chiaromonte was involved with editorially between 1956 and 1967. A number of articles by Caffi were posthumously published in the journal.

More recently, Amanda Swain has been responsible for a number of articles on Chiaromonte. In 2024 she published "Utopia in New York: Nicola Chiaromonte and the New York Intellectuals' "Superstition of Science"", an interesting piece, that amongst other things registers that

---

61 Abel, Op. Cit., p. 45.

62 Swain, "Utopia in New York...", p. 411.

63 Marco Bresciani, "Socialism, Fascism and Anti-Totalitarianism". There is also material on Chiaromonte in Bresciani's book on *Giustizia e Libertà, Learning from History*.

64 Chiara Morbi and Paola Carlucci, "Beyond the Cold War: *Tempo Presente* in Italy", in Giles Scott-Smith, Charlotte Lerg, *Campaigning Culture and the Global Cold War: the Journals of the Congress for Cultural Freedom*, London, Palgrave MacMillan, 2017.

Chiaromonte and Caffi both appeared regularly in *Instead*.[65] Also in 2024 she published "'One of the last secret maestros': Nicola Chiaromonte between Europe and America".[66] Finally, in 2025, she published, with Valerio Angeletti, "The *Lampadophorous*: Paolo Milano, Nicola Chiaromonte and the politics of friendship".[67] This interesting article, as well as considering the relationship between Milano[68] and Chiaromonte, also notes the impact of Caffi on Milano, who like Chiaromonte and Albert Camus "would look after Caffi before his death".[69] It points to the role of Meyer Schapiro in introducing Chiaromonte to Dwight Macdonald.[70] This recent burst of historical scholarship has added greatly to our knowledge of Chiaromonte.

In conclusion as editor of the book I would like to make clear that the overwhelming bulk of the footnotes are editorial. On the very few occasions that Caffi himself added a footnote to an article, this is flagged clearly at the start of the footnote. I have attempted to reproduce the articles as faithfully to the original as possible, which includes several typos and formatting peculiarities. I'd like to thank Cayce Jamil for his belief in the importance of this book and his work in assisting the editorial production of the book, and Alberto Castelli for his encouragement and the production of the Afterword. Daniele Basi, Amanda Swain, and Gregory Sumner all encouraged and helped the production of the book. Robert Jackson and Sarah Goodman provided invaluable assistance in tracking down copies of *Instead*. Mykell Gates Jamil produced the covers of the book, for which many thanks. As ever, I must thank Kath for her assistance and forbearance, and her enthusiasm for our trips to Père Lachaise to ensure that Andrea Caffi remains remembered.

Mike Tyldesley

---

65 Swain, "Utopia in New York...", p. 414.

66 Amanda Swain, "'One of the last secret maestros': Nicola Chiaromonte between Europe and America", *Journal of Modern Italian Studies*, Vol. 29 (2024), No. 2, pp. 127–143.

67 Valerio Angeletti, Amanda Swain, "The *Lampadophorous*: Paolo Milano, Nicola Chiaromonte and the politics of Friendship", *Forum Italicum*, Vol. 59 (2025),1, pp. 3-20. *Lampadophorous* is a term for lamp-bearer.

68 Paolo Milano (1904–1988), Italian literary critic.

69 Angeletti and Swain, Op. Cit., p. 15, footnote 13.

70 Angeletti and Swain, Op. Cit., p. 9.

The Automatization of European People[71]

Editorial note: I have taken the liberty of giving to the following two letters from France a title perhaps more pretentious than their author would approve. My excuse must be that they seem to me to be the most profound analysis, in intellectual and in moral terms, of the psychology of postwar Europe which I have yet encountered. Their author, incidentally, is one of those to whom the readers of POLITICS are sending regular food packages.

I.

Dear D.M.[72]:

You can scarcely imagine into what wretchedness (moral and physical) we are sinking; always the level is lower; for if the mass of goods (or commodities) has increased a bit, the inequality of distribution is constantly more marked. In the sphere of material existence, the distance between prices and salaries (or other doles to the working class) is ever more shocking. In the sphere of cultural "goods," the possibilities of action (or even of participation in some action) are monopolized by the groups that have the support of the "government parties," and nobody can pass muster without pledging his allegiance.

To illustrate the first point: a fairly decent meal in a restaurant runs here to at least 300 francs. In Paris, the prices are even higher. Now most of the workers, and lower-salaried employees (not to speak of the unemployed), live on less than 4,000 francs a month. The question: how do they survive? seems to me idle. When I was in Russia in 1920–1922, I saw something analogous to the present case: it seems you cannot kill off everybody, not all at once. I have heard, for example, that despite the most ferocious techniques, the American sanitation corps has not succeeded in killing all the mosquitoes in the Arles sector, and I will bet you anything you please that they will never get to the last louse in

---

71 Article published in *politics* magazine, November 1945.

72 This part of the article is based on a letter from Caffi to Dwight Macdonald, editor of *politics*. Gregory Sumner, in his *Dwight Macdonald and the politics Circle*, discusses this article at some length, p. 77 et seq.

Montauban.[73] There are countless levels of the liveable, and the thought of survival suggests miraculous expedients; last winter children died "like flies" in France, in Italy, in Greece and elsewhere; but there are a great many left. Beings decaying before one's eyes, accustomed to unwholesome and repugnant "food," who have given up washing themselves except in summer in the rivers; who dwell—if one may use such a word—heaped in hovels, and travel, stacked in ever denser piles, in broken-down conveyances; who can bring to their regular work and social life (in which I include the political demonstrations they attend) nothing more than a mechanical assent; such are the components of the *population*. I underline this word because De Gaulle has recently declared that his regime will not rest on the people, but on the population...

As for this second phenomena—the monopoly of ideological activity—this is made possible by the censorship (officially non-existent), by the rationing of paper, the prohibition of periodicals in foreign languages, but in the main by the pressure exerted by massive groups on all dissident minorities. Naturally, there is always a way of triumphing over material obstacles: paper can be got on the black market, presses can easily escape the not-too-diligent surveillance; but this requires means which are possessed by the faithful of the former Vichy regime and are totally lacking to those who persist in being rebellious, and whom the Stalinists denounce as "the Hitlero-Trotzkyite Fifth Column."

But these pecuniary difficulties do not explain the paralysis of spontaneous, daring, passionate initiatives, the absence of that swarming of "clubs" and plans however naive, bizarre, messianic, which characterize a truly revolutionary ferment. It is rather a question of the psychological inertia of the people. What I have in mind is not the famous "passivity" of the masses," (*sic*) who by definition are sheeplike and simplistic, but the strange will to obey, to be subject to a hierarchy and *not have to reflect*, shown by those who would ordinarily be the active nuclei of the nation and form the cadres of the organized parties. What is clamored for is "unity" (of the Resistance, of "anti-fascists," of the Republic); the fusion at no matter what cost of the Socialist and

---

73 Arles is a canton on the coast of southern France. Montauban is a commune
  in southern France to the west of Arles.

communist parties, of the CGT[74] and the clerical trade unions; the maximum centralization of the State apparatus; and the maximum homogeneity in the nation. (I refer to France with its conglomerate "movements," and to Italy with its six coalition parties; I know nothing at all about how matters stand in this respect in other countries; but among the Spaniards I have detected a like trend). There is an overwhelming desire to jettison difficult problems, intransigent principles, responsibility for one's own consciousness. This is probably not a mere effect of fatigue and under-nourishment, nor of the fascination of totalitarian forms (though these factors have some weight). There is something here which relates to the forces you noted in your remarks on Popular Culture—the habits of automatism, of *zusammenmarschieren*[75], of responding to slogans that are as imperative as they are trivial, habits which the cinema, the radio, the newspaper headlines, the rationalization of work and pleasure, the tyranny of schedules, have spread and developed to a maximum point. There is an almost complete dislocation of the "norms" in accordance with which one judges his fellows and moves towards or with them; no real relation between "mores" and "morals," between immediate, intimate experience and the formulas or schemes (more or less abstract) which purport to express the reality of the world in which we live. For example, compounds like "Nation-country-State," or "technological progress-civilization-humanism," all such "realities" are today a kind of indigestible and quality-less broth, made of *ersatz*[76] and false syntheses, but which must be gulped down and then praised to the skies, if one is to avoid an agonising and unsustainable hunger, the frightful condition of having to live, spiritually, on nothing, and being, so to speak, left naked in an empty space.

This apathy and disorder—not of the mass, I repeat (the mass of the population want only peace and goods)—but of what was known as the "people" from 1789 to 1914 in Europe, and which was called "society"

---

74 *Confédération Générale du Travail* (General Confederation of Labour). A trade union centre, and at the time Caffi was writing, the largest in France. In 1945 it was becoming increasingly dominated by the French Communist Party (PCF), and in 1948 its pre-war non-Communist leadership around Léon Jouhaux withdrew, and formed the rival *Force Ouvrière* (Workers' Power) union centre. Both organisations are still in existence.

75 Literally: 'marching together'.

76 i.e.: 'fake', 'substitute', 'not real or genuine'.

in the France of the 18th century and in the Russia of the whole 19th century—this apathy, I say, has been carefully nurtured by the Stalinist propaganda and the organization of "popular fronts" under the control of the communists. Militant communists have explained to me that such things as "ideologies" and spontaneous uprisings of the oppressed are out of date, and that what is needful now is a big army, well-officered, mobilizable at the first signal (for ends which it would be useless to explain in advance to each soldier or even to each non-com), and which must be kept ready and above all disciplined, so that no provocation will cause it to budge until commanded to act. The implication is that revolution could be set off, but its potential threat is valuable as a means of pressure and blackmail. For the moment, Moscow's politics requires the complete immobility of these forces, but on this or that day, in such and such a place, trouble may have value, and it will be only necessary to give the word for violence to break out. The men who become recruits out of a sincere desire for revolution must accept the notion that a single mind, not theirs, but thinking for them all, will determine the favorable moment for the great trial, and that it would be foolish and even criminal to become impatient simply because D-Day has been put off indefinitely.

For the moment, it seems that the main concern of those who control this streamlined apparatus is to prevent any attempt at federation by the people of Europe (vetoed alike are the proposals for Scandinavian unity, the most modest attempts at a Balkan or Danubian Federation; there was a watchful campaign against the very vague project of a French-Dutch-Belgian Customs Union having ties with Britain.) This implies a methodical stimulation to the various nationalisms in their meanest forms.

In domestic policies (in France and in Italy at least) there is the usual double talk: 1) appeals for *l'union sacrée*[77] of all "patriots," the only stipulation being that they glorify the USSR, "our powerful ally"; 2) a sterile excitation of the hatred felt for certain "traitors" or profiteers, so as to persuade the public, that all would go well if some fifty people were jailed, or if certain others were shot instead of being given five year

---

77 A 'Sacred Union'. In the war-time context, a wide alliance of both left and right.

sentences. In this way all serious critical examination of the real problem is conjured away. The agitation is perpetual, and always short of breath...

You are right to be pleased that your circulation is up to 5,000 (which means, I suppose, three times as many readers). Candide would say perhaps, thinking of the two hundred million bipeds who can read English; "it is not very much." But I would reply with Martin: "it is a great deal."[78] You have opened a breach in a Bastille far more formidable and oppressive than the Nazi *Festung Europa*[79], battered down only at the cost of twenty or thirty million human lives. We cannot expect much in the near future, and I should even say that dazzling successes (of socialism, for example) would frighten me—I would fear a repetition of that cascade of "ultra-democratic" constitutions that we saw showered over Europe in 1919.

What is important is that there be a lighted torch, like yours, around which to rally..

EUROPEAN

July 22, 1945.

II.

Dear N.[80]:

At the beginning of 1944, S.[81] (who was then doing very dangerous work for the Resistance) came to see me. Among other things, he

---

78 In Voltaire's 1759 novel *Candide,* Candide is a sheltered and naïve young man while Martin is a pessimistic rational scholar.

79 i.e: 'Fortress Europe'.

80 N. was Caffi's friend Nicola Chiaromonte. The text upon which this letter is based is now available in the original French and an Italian translation in Marco Bresciani, *«Cosa Sperare?» Il Carteggio tra Andrea Caffi e Nicola Chiaromonte: un dialogo sulla rivoluzione (1932-1955).* For this letter see pp. 174-181 (French) and pp. 181-190 (Italian; the substantial footnotes are to the Italian text.)

81 "S." was in fact Mario Levi. See Bresciani, *«Cosa Sperare?»* p. 182, Footnote 70. For Caffi's work with Mario Levi in the 1930s, when both had been involved in *Giustizia e Libertà* Italian anti-fascist movement in Paris, see M. Tyldesley, *Liberate and Federate,* pp. 25–30. Levi's sister also wrote about Caffi (who she called 'Cafi') and his connection to Levi in Natalia Ginzburg, *Family Lexicon.*

challenged my views about Russia. Naturally, I was defeated. I was unable to explain clearly how a heroic nationalistic psychosis, accompanied by gigantic holocausts (*Opfer fallen, weder Lamm noch Stier, aber Menschenopfer unerhoert*—"sacrificial victims are being slaughtered—neither lambs nor steers, but humans, fall in numbers untold") had driven into the background any coherent vision of social justice. While on the other hand, it was left for the future historian to evaluate how much real spontaneity went into those offerings.

In the course of a subsequent visit, S. expounded to me the following thesis: in the present world, nothing is possible if a State (and a superlatively strong State at that) does not take the initiative. Impossible to fight the Germans without the parachutists, without the millions of francs sent from London, without the directions given by the Intelligence Service, etc. The resistance wouldn't have had one single submachine-gun if it had not accepted the outside support (i.e. the direction) of certain Governments. On my part, I felt inclined to uphold a utopian view very similar to the one developed by "Gallicus" in POLITICS.[82] I thought that, from the point of view of Europe's future, the aim to have in mind should rather have been that of a true insurrection of the European peoples harassing and undermining the *Herrenvolk*[83] with their own means. I willingly admit (now) the weakness of my argument. I was then haunted by the recollection of the contempt with which, in 1904–1905, in Russia, our revolutionary organizations had rejected all offers of money and weapons from Japanese emissaries whose aim was to quicken the general defeatism of the Russian people in order to win easier victories for the armies of the Mikado.[84] I believe that Pilsudski[85] and a few Finns did not offer such a categorical refusal, and I do remember that there was some wavering in Lenin's circle: *Realpolitik* first...) (*sic*). But above all, I did not then give enough consideration to the most crushing objection of all: namely that with the methods employed at Auschwitz and Belsen (of which at that time we had a knowledge which was not only vague, but also weakened by fits of incredulity) Hitler could very well have destroyed the

---

82 Apparently a reference to an article by "Gallicus" in the January 1945 edition
   of *politics*, called "The liberals' 'indispensible man': Hitler".
83 Colloquially: 'Master race'
84 Mikado was the formal title of the emperor of Japan.
85 Marshal Josef Pilsudski (1867–1935), Polish nationalist leader, and member
   of Polish Socialist Party until 1918.

seed of the opposition before it could give any fruit at all. Nevertheless, to reject that hazardous way could not mean anything but to resign oneself to "gaullism," and to the rest. It seemed to me that one should at least be clear about what "gaullism," and the rest, meant. But, of course, since S. was then engaged in perilous action, he [was] psychologically justified in not asking himself too many questions.

Anyway, shortly after the liberation, S.'s position appeared to be that only the Stalinists (with the powerful support of the victorious Red Army) could do anything at all in a revolutionary direction. As for myself, I foresaw (and I think that on this at least I was not entirely wrong) a convergence of militarism and of Stalinist demagogy toward the following double aim: 1) a reinforcement of police control inside every European state; 2) the suppression of any tendency toward a "European Federation." And I think that by now S. himself has very little confidence left in the P.C.[86] as "defender of the little people against the trusts."

As for the resistance movement as a whole, in my opinion one must distinguish between the "Maquis" and the "Resistance." I think that to have an idea of the "Maquis," you could recall, without too much risk of being led astray, your own experience in Spain, at the beginning of the Civil War. In fact, in our region, the Spanish guerrilleros have been without any doubt both the backbone of, and the most numerous element in, the insurrection.

But one cannot help feeling embarrassed in dealing with such matters. The bodies—bodies of young martyrs infinitely worthy of our love—are still there, still warm. In their presence, it sounds almost blasphemous to give way to the sadness one feels in seeing once more how youth can indeed be *"a tout asservie"* (exploited for anything). Because, after all, didn't the dictators themselves find myriads of young souls as enthusiastic as these, and (one feels compelled to add) not less pure either? Do not now the official orators of all official commemorations extol the fraternity which united, during the resistance, the young men brought up by the "Action Francaise"[87] with the pupils of the late Komintern? Once he is ready to kneel to the idol Nation, Liberty becomes nothing more than its pale satellite, and, from then on, everything is simple. Must one rejoice

---

86 (French) Communist Party, ie *Parti Communiste Français* (PCF)
87 French proto-fascist organisation.

or worry over the fact that the French as well as the Italian Resistance movements have adopted unreservedly the kind of pragmatism preached by the late Mussolini: "Let us act first, ideas will come later, by themselves?" This is not an idle metaphysical question, or a pedantic query about the priority of thought. It is rather that one is terror-stricken by such a massive utilization of the most precious human qualities for ends that are to say the least problematic. The philosophy of the "absurd," so nobly and so subtly understood by men like Albert Camus, is not meant for mass-consumption. Hence, it is by the use of vulgar fetishes that the Mahomets[88] of our time form "armies of believers" which will then rush on to death like bees to the honeycomb. The human bombs of the Japanese appear to be the final, normalised, form of such techniques of government.

After which, one has to mention the very old story that the blood shed in amphitheatres and prisons makes very good cement to fasten the power and the prosperity of simoniac bishops and despots. "We are the '*party des fusillés.*'[89] Hence, bow very low, ye masses, before Cachin, Marty, Thorez, Duclos[90], who miraculously survived the deadly battle." There is a miserable competition going on, between parties, and also between nations, each exhibiting its own list of martyrs in order to get a full profit from it.

Resistance to totalitarianism will remain as an imperishable honor to mankind. It was to individuals and groups of very dissimilar origin and nature (*sic*), and it was carried out with makeshift means, under circumstances which were mostly atrocious. The final result can even be considered providential, but in itself it is certainly not a conquest: men have remained men (or nearly so), they have not become robots, they have not all perished in the crematoriums of Hitlerland. The resistance— with a capital R, and an accompaniment of trumpets, drums, manifestoes, bids for profitable jobs, and plans for new totalitarian arrangements—is a very elastic compound of sincere messianic hopes, demagogical totems and taboos, very noble and very abject ambitions, dreams of liberty, and will-to-power. It is an artificial mythology choking and perverting

---

88 An older, Anglicized spelling for the prophet Muhammad.
89 Literally, 'party of the shot', a term used by the PCF to enhance its Resistance credentials.
90 Contemporary PCF leaders.

authentic "epos,"[91] which is born in the depths of consciousness and in the real communion of a people.

It seems clear that, after the lamentable comedy of the Etats Generaux of July 14th[92], the re-establishment of military hierarchy (with the exclusion or the humiliation of the FFI[93]), and the majestic reappearance in the limelight of Messrs. Herriot, Daladier, Reynaud & Co.[94], the chances of a Resistance still embodying something of the true spirit of the resistance of the French people to Hitlerism and Petainism are very slim indeed. The people cannot understand an indefinitely prolonged resistance, in the same way that they cannot understand a "permanent revolution." After all the struggle and the suffering, the people do not ask either for honors or (much less) for the continuation of an exceptional strain. They want a rest, enough to eat, to get married, and to be able to dance and to go to the movies. Of course, if they do not get these things, there will be trouble again. But the exhaustion is such that one can legitimately wonder if, given a moderate amount of normalcy, an authoritarian regime would not be able to organize a triumphant plebiscite in its favour...

EUROPEAN

Sept. 3, 1945.

---

91 Literally an epic, but in this context something like 'myth'.

92 An attempt by the Resistance organisations—the local liberation committees created by the *Conseil Nationale de la Résistance* (CNR: National Council of the Resistance)—to create some sort of political and moral leadership for France. Its full title was *Etats Généraux de la Renaissance Française*, and it produced *cahiers de la Résistance*. As James D Wilkinson notes in his interesting brief account of it (which bears out Caffi's pretty much 'on the spot' analysis), the terminology in effect laid claim to the symbolism of the French Revolution. (See James D Wilkinson, *The Intellectual Resistance in Europe*, Cambridge (Mass), Harvard University Press, 1981, pp. 75–76). It was, according to both Caffi and Wilkinson, a clear failure.

93 *Forces françaises de l'intérieur*, the French Forces of the Interior: Formal name for French Resistance fighters in the latter part of the Second World War.

94 Pre-war 'moderate' or 'centrist' politicians whose opposition to collaboration with the Germans meant that they were able to return to politics after the war.

Towards a Socialist Program[95]

The Editor writes in the August issue: "We must 'get' the modern National State before it 'gets' us".

I think this is indeed the question.

Along this line, too, is the conclusion of Victor Serge's[96] letter in the same issue: "Contemporary socialism should frankly recognize *its past mistakes* in this field and should put itself forward as the *uncompromising* defender of human life and human rights".

But we must have no illusions about the effort we must exert against our own natures if we would rid ourselves of the usual way—assumed to be the only way—of looking at the political and economic organization of modern society, and also of conceiving of that entity which is *the nation* (an entity that is "social" according to Gurvitch[97], spiritual according to Mazzini and Renan, linked with "popular sovereignty" according to the Jacobins, taken as a natural division of mankind by Marxism). Let us not deceive ourselves. The attitude that seemed so natural to Montesquieu ("I am French by chance, but a man by necessity") is most difficult to realize in practice today, after the French Revolution, romanticism, the national unifications of the 19th century, and the famous right of peoples to self-determination.

---

95 Article published in *politics* magazine, December 1945. It is based upon a letter from Caffi to N. Chiaromonte sent in August 1945 (and thus earlier than "The Automatization of European People"). See Marco Bresciani, *«Cosa Sperare?» Il Carteggio tra Andrea Caffi e Nicola Chiaromonte: un dialogo sulla rivoluzione (1932-1955)*. For this letter see pp. 165-169 (French) and pp. 169-174 (Italian, with footnotes).

96 Victor Serge (1890–1947), Russian anti-Stalinist socialist exile—at this time in Mexico—writer. See his *Memoirs of a Revolutionary, 1901-1941*, New York, New York Review of Books Classics, 2012, and Susan Weissman, *Victor Serge: The Course is Set on Hope*, London, Verso, 2001.

97 Georges Gurvitch (1894–1965), Russian-French sociologist, and an important influence on Caffi, whom he probably met in Paris before the Second World War. See M. Tyldesley, *Liberate and Federate*.

Jean Malaquais'[98] execution of the wretched Aragon was very good. But what can we do about the "honest bundle of sentiments" of the patriotic Moldavian or Batavian? Or the patriotism of Leon Blum, or that of the editors of *Combat,* who are also fascinated by "wide human horizons"?

Robert Anders[99] criticizes Beveridge's economic proposals with great clarity, and yet what he himself would substitute for Beveridgism is a socialist economic plan which seems to respect *national* lines.

I vote with both hands for Dwight Macdonald's demonstration of the totalitarian nature of much modern liberal thinking. And yet the problem remains: If the six million Swedes form a geographical and political "organism", and if the 160 million Russians form another such compact and united "organism", how to guarantee the secure existence of the weak Sweden next door to the mighty Russia—short of a universal moral conversion, or of the enforcement of a system of international police (in which case, *Quis Custodiet Custodes?*[100])

The idea that "the workers have no fatherland", like the older concept of the "citizen of the world", seems either antiquated or else of so abstract a nature as to be inapplicable to our everyday experience.

Religious movements—compacts of emotion, fraternity and spiritual culture—have hardened into Churches (the Egyptian hierarchy, Brahmanism, Islam, Roman Catholicism, and other established Churches). They represented an amalgam of moral teachings, an apparatus of coercion, and economic power. We know well what this has meant in terms of the subjugation of man, the perversion of culture, and the profanation of religious feeling itself. Greece never knew such forms of dogmatism, submitting the soul and the body to the same police control. Hence it was the revival of Greek thought that helped western man to revolt against ecclesiastical tyranny. We have succeeded, although very incompletely, in curbing the Churches by forcing them to accept the status of private associations, by curtailing their riches, by taking away

---

98 A reference to Jean Malaquais' article in *politics,* August 1945, "Louis Aragon, or the Professional Patriot". Aragon was a leading PCF intellectual, Malaquais an inveterate French anti-Stalinist leftist.
99 Reference to Robert Anders, "Can Capitalism be Humanized?", again in *politics,* August 1945.
100 "Who guards the guards?"

from them the support of the "secular arm". But for religious idols, other idols have been substituted, not less nefarious.

Many modern historians—not only German—have reproached the Hellenes because of their obdurate opposition to the unified national State which Philip of Macedonia and his successors, and Titus Flamininus after them, so generously wanted to impose on Hellas. Still, a Greek was fully and proudly conscious of his native tongue, of his culture, of his ethnic characteristics. But a Greek would never have understood what we Europeans have accepted as a perfectly natural fact since the 16th century: that a man could alienate his humanity for the greater glory and splendor of his "ethnicity".

Modern despotism in its successive stages—Louis XIV, Frederick William I, the Committee of Public Safety and Napoleon, Bismarck, Hitler and Stalin—is based on an amalgam similar to that on which theocracy rests. The moral and intellectual values of the *nation* seem unable to exist if not founded on the monopoly of a territory, which in its turn requires an increasingly strong State and an economic organisation. From mercantilism to "socialism in one country", this economic organisation has always shown a definite tendency toward "autarchy", while, on the other hand, the opposite tendency, economic expansion culminating in imperialism, is just as nationalistic, "fair play" being proposed only insofar as one is perfectly assured that he is the stronger.

This is the bundle (the *fasces*[101]...) that has to be undone, if we mean what we say when we affirm that we do not want man to be devoured by the National State. The problem appears to be how to dissociate the nation from the government of the territory, and this from the organisation of economic life.

It seems evident that the more differentiated the systems of relations between men and groups, the more concretely is freedom guaranteed in human society. There is, however, one condition: that any bond between the individual and a group be voluntarily constituted and easily rescinded.

If the nation, conceived as the community of people speaking and "cultivating" the same language and united by common memories, could become a private association deprived of any power to force people to

---

101 The root word for Fascism.

join it or prevent them from leaving it, the real "national values" would not fare any worse than true religious values in a really "free" Church.

Modern technology requires more than ever that the circulation of commodities, of men, of ideas, take place without any hindrance. It should be a fundamental article of the law of nations that no authority—be it local, national or international—has the power (except in a few well defined cases such as that of sanitary quarantine) to prevent the passage of any person to any point on earth. The government of the territory (subdivided into small autonomous units) should be entrusted to all the adults who have been residing on it, let's say for the last three years, without any consideration for the country in which they were born, their language, their race. etc.

After which, the most difficult problem would remain: the organization of economic life. Economic life is inconceivable today except on a world scale. The danger would be great, if an enormous economic power were to be concentrated in a few directing centers. On the other hand, there seems to be no question as to the inadvisability of entrusting either the States or a coalition of them (into some kind of League of Nations) with the direction of world-economy. Again, we should take into consideration a plurality of associations deprived of any power of coercion, except for the unavoidable pressure of massive majorities and of purely economic power. Railroads, mining centers, and other essential economic structures, should be organized into large boards where 1) the technicians; 2) the Council of workers; 3) the representatives of the consumers, would cooperate (or come into conflict) in the management of the respective concerns. There should be a world federation of the labor unions; and cooperatives should also have a world organization.

The "federal principle" should be the basic principle of all these organizations, with a maximum of autonomy at the bottom and a minimum of unrestricted power at the top. In such a way, the freedom of the individual would be protected as much as it is humanly possible. And we should never forget that freedom cannot exist without some disorder. *A free man creates disorder.* There is no "pre-established harmony" between the maximum of human freedom and the highest efficiency of an economic or juridical organization. If we think of economic activity in terms of sheer efficiency, then, of course, we cannot have freedom.

In terms of the present wretched conditions, all this is Utopia, of course. The real question, however, seems to be if from a socialist, humanistic, and rational, point of view it is possible to think according to lines essentially different from these. I would be contradicting some of my firmest convictions if I implied in any way that I am thinking of some kind of "ideal constitution" into which the human cattle should be penned by physical violence, or by the not less brutal means of demagogical arguments. Problems, conflicts, the tragedies caused by misunderstanding and *Hubris* will go on as long as there will be men. The question is not how to eliminate sorrow and conflict from human life, but, for each one of us, in what direction to think and to strive.

Socialism, the search for Justice as well as for human happiness, cannot be satisfied anymore with the Marxian notions of 1) class struggle inside each nation; 2) seizure of State power in order first to utilize it and then to scrap it. The most peaceful civilian is nowadays exposed to dangers that are probably greater than those faced by the soldier in battle. Hence the immediate and resolute attitude of each and every person is today far more important than any question of political strategy. We must do everything we can to bring about the disintegration of the compact State-territory-Nation.

Politics has been right in paying much attention to the conscientious objectors. One of its correspondents has said of the Germans (how accurately I could not tell, but it seems significant in any case): "it was the most intelligent thing that the Germans could do, lacking, as they did, the physical power to overthrow Hitler, but being able to force him to suicide by becoming *a nation of Gandhis...*". On the other hand, it is reasonably sure that the Italian people brought about Mussolini's downfall with their refusal to cooperate with him.

Would it be far-fetched to consider conscientious objection, passive resistance, refusal to obey and to cooperate as new forms, however intensified and charged with a greater potential of individual responsibility, of that old method of struggle, which the proletariat discovered instinctively and which brought them so many essential conquests: the *strike*?

It is to give a clear direction to such an effort, whose signs are still rather dim and confused, that every socialist and every group of socialists should work, by developing some fundamental principles to be followed consistently in private life as well as in all public manifestations.

We should come to an agreement on the radical refusal to submit to the idolatrous trinity "Nation-Fatherland-State".

The International, conceived as a compound of nations, has been proved illusory. A new International should be based on the radical negation of the Nation insofar as it is an organism armed with means of compulsion.

Since 1789, the Nation has become a divinity. We must desecrate it.

As for the State, once it is deprived of the national sacrament, it becomes a machinery, and nothing else. As such, the only proper answer to its unbearable claims is sabotage.

But our third principle should be: final, irrevocable renunciation of any form of organized violence.

EUROPEAN

Is a Revolutionary War a Contradiction in Terms?
A Letter from "European"[102]

In his article, "Why Politics?"[103], in the first issue of POLITICS, Dwight Macdonald sketches out his attitude towards the Soviet Union and the war that was then in process. The notion of "bureaucratic collectivism" as a third alternative to capitalism and socialism seems to me perfectly right, and clearly defined. The attitude toward the war, on the other hand, appears difficult to found on a consistent line of reasoning.

It might be that war, whatever its motives and aims, is an essentially unacceptable fact from a socialist point of view. At the same time, since we are living men, inescapably involved in the common fate of our fellow men, we cannot "simply draw aside and say: it's none of our business". But then one should add that it will be forever impossible to find in war any element whatsoever of "our business". We can submit to fate with dignity; save our own soul, help a few friends to save theirs. But that will be all.

After having justly refused to accept as legitimate an attitude of "critical support", the Editor goes on to say that "The proper policy would have been to insist on taking the fight against Hitler into the hands of the workers".

It would seem as if, at this point, the "hands of the workers" helped us to slip from reality into phraseology. The brave workers are millions of men and women who, we have every right to assume, yearn for truth and justice, and (in moments of great fervor) are fully capable of facing the cruellest tortures rather than submit to slavery. But, *at the present moment*, it may be a bit demagogical merely on the basis of some ideal image concerning their "historical mission" to attribute to them real competence in the art of government, State affairs, and the handling of several other technical and spiritual matters.

The struggle against Hitler, in the form it had inexorably taken in 1940, required a complex strategy of tanks, airplanes, submarines, General

---

102 Article published in *politics*, April 1946.
103 Dwight Macdonald, "Why "POLITICS"?", *politics,* (no. 1), February 1944.

Staffs, armies, fifth columns; the organization of a constant and well-ordered flow of supplies to this machinery; the creation of an artificial "morale" to keep the human herd rushing onto death; the terrorisation of the conquered people; the ruthless exploitation of every ounce of human effort that could be exploited.

How could all this have been in the "hands of the workers"? By entrusting it to leaders more capable than the fascist leaders, or at least as capable as them? But then these leaders would have had to be armed with powers as wide, and practically as uncontrollable, as those of Hitler's or Stalin's lieutenants. There is not such a thing as a "socialist" (or "proletarian") way of waging war, of opposing massacre with massacre.

A revolt of the workers against Churchill in 1940 would not have involved simply the "risk of a Nazi victory", but its certainty. In time of war, a revolution (I insist, a revolution, not a coup d'Etat) is unavoidably defeatist in its effects, if not in its avowed intentions (Russia in 1917; Austria-Hungary in 1918; Italy in 1943).

No revolution is in fact possible if the State apparatus is not wrecked. Lenin thought that, while falling from the hands of the dethroned tyrants into those of the new conquerors, the apparatus would remain in fairly good working order. This has been refuted by the very experience of the Bolsheviks: for several years, Russia did not have either an army or an administration. It was precisely what made the years 1917–1922, for all their horror and suffering, years of hope and faith. The peasants did not submit to any rule except direct violence, and only as long as a detachment of Reds remained in the village; badly armed and equipped as they were (I happen to have seen something of them), Denikin's or Youdenitch's[104] bands were able to reach the outskirts of Moscow and St. Petersburg; Makhno[105] wielded a military power equal to that of Trotzky. Once the State, the army, the police were reconstituted, the real revolution, the ferment of the autonomous Soviets, the enthusiasm of the workers became nothing but vanishing phantoms. The same had happened to the "Jacobin conquest" in 1794, in spite of the fact that the

---

104 Anton Denikin (1872–1947) and Nikolai Youdenitch (1862–1933), White Army commanders in the Russian Civil War.
105 Nestor Makhno (1888–1934), commander of the Revolutionary Insurgent Army of Ukraine (anarchist) during the Russian Civil War.

Jacobins could rely on many experienced bourgeois administrators. War invariably kills revolution. The idea that there can be such a thing as a "revolutionary war" is based on a fundamental confusion against which Proudhon fought a losing battle. But Marx took the idea over as a matter of course from the Romantic tradition, making of it a necessary dialectical step.

"*Vive la commune de Paris—ses mitrailleuses et ses fusils*" (Long live the Paris Commune—its machine-guns and its rifles)—So went the song of the Parisian workers. But precisely its machine-guns and its rifles eliminated every hope of the Paris Commune's becoming what it had wanted to be. The Commune could have defeated Versailles. The result would have been a change of insignia on barracks, Police Headquarters, jails, etc., with the possible injection of a dose of democracy (i.e., in the best hypothesis, a small amount of sloppiness) into the machinery of coercion.

If socialism has to mean a true emancipation of man, we have to start by rejecting as a major absurdity any notion of a war waged by socialists, or of a State managed in the name of socialism.

Never has a people defeated the State that oppressed it by force of arms. In *De la Guerre et de la Paix*[106], Proudhon distinguished the kind of force that is at play in modern society, and in a real revolution, from the brutal Force that decides wars between nations, which he considered a relic of barbarism.

In all successful revolutions, the decisive factor has been a "moral" or "psychological" one—the one thanks to which the always superior armament of the State has been rendered useless. If the guns of the Bastille had fired, July 14th, 1789, in Paris, [it] would have been the same as January 22, 1905, in St. Petersburg. In March, 1917, the Cossacks refused to charge the people. If the soldiers of the Duke of Ragusa had obeyed their Marshal, the Three Glorious Day (*sic*) of 1830 would have ended like the sorrowful days of June, 1848.

There is not a single example of the people's being victorious against a force organized by the state and ready to support the rulers. What I myself have seen of the evacuation of Southern France by the Germans, and what I have heard of the evacuation of Paris and of Milan by the

---

106 *War and Peace* (1861)

same, confirms such an opinion. The Spanish guerrillas against Napoleon would have met the same fate as the Vendee[107], had Wellington not been there with his regular soldiers and his gold. A guerrilla force on its own—that is Warsaw in August, 1944.

The illusion of an insurrection victorious by force of arms is similar to, and also connected with, the conventional XIX century view of "military glory". Norton Cru[108] maintains (and he seems to be right) that we cannot get anywhere near a true picture of what Napoleon's battles really were like because all the witnesses have falsified their accounts according to the preconceived notion they had accepted of the phenomenon: "combat between two armies". The history of revolutionary combats should be revised from a similar point of view. Marx, and especially Engels (whose competence in strategic matters has been particularly admired), never conceived the possibility of looking at the fact "battle" from a point of view other than the point of view of Clausewitz.[109] For them, such insights into the naked reality of the "historical" as Stendhal's Waterloo or Tolstoi's Austerlitz, remained entirely out of reach.

Of course, the revolution (popular insurrection, collapse of a machinery of oppression on account of the desertion of its agents) can bring in its wake a civil war, with all that a war implies of military organization, stern discipline, regular battles, etc. But it will then be the struggle between two State organizations, not that of a people against a ruling caste. On both sides, the people will get killed under the direction of a caste, old or new, of officers, generals, and political rulers. There is no doubt that, since we are democrats and socialists, we will be right in preferring the victory of the Lenin-Trotzky state to that of the Koltchak-Denikin state; of the Tcheka installed by Bela Kun in the Crimea to that of Wrangel's[110] "Kontr' Rasviedka" which ravaged the same peninsula—in much the same sense as we could have preferred Grant's soldiery in New Orleans to Lee's in Kentucky. To enlist in the International Brigade in order to fight

---

107 A revolt against the Revolutionary government in 1793 in the area of Eastern France called Vendée.

108 Possibly French writer Jean Norton Cru (1879-1949).

109 Carl von Clausewitz (1780-1831), 18th and 19th century Prussian general and military theorist.

110 Bela Kun (1886-1938), leader of the Hungarian Soviet Republic, 1919. Pyotr Wrangel (1878-1928) and Alexander Kolchak (1874-1920), White Commanders in the Russian Civil War.

Franco's hordes might well appear to be one's imperative duty. But is there much difference between such choices and the sympathy for the Boers against Britain; for Ethiopia against Italy; for the Greeks against the Turks at Domokos in 1898; for France, not much a republic then, against Prussia, in 1871? Or, in more recent times, the anxious expectation with which we waited for General Alexander to replace Marshall Kesselring[111] in Milan, and for a Soviet Marshal to eject a Nazi governor from Poland?

We are confronted, over and over again, with the same irreducible duality of feelings: "It is none of our business", and, nevertheless, "de nostra re agitur"—it *is* our business . . . A fine point for an existential philosopher, with his subtle dialectic of being and nothingness, absolute commitment and failure, metaphysical freedom and inescapable historical situation.

Stating his point of view on the war, the Editor also wrote: "If ever there was a chance for socialism in Britain, it was in the period from Dunkirk to the fall of Tobruk".

I think that this assertion is seriously challenged by a passage from *Mass Observation,* as quoted by Mr. Orlansky (*Politics* - December 1944)[112]: "An investigation in 1942 showed about as much criticism of the Labour Party as of the Conservatives. Asked whether they felt that *any party* would get things done as they wanted, 64% thought that *no* existing party would do so...".

When the numerical majority of a people feel so bitterly disoriented, the probability of a revolutionary explosion is very slim. Revolution always requires a long labor of great expectations, and a great deal of robust faith in certain men and in certain doctrines. The man who declares that he has no confidence in any of the existing parties is by the same token confessing to a feeling of isolation and a very poor hope that his discontent might have a positive outcome. And one should also take into account the paralysing effect of patriotic anguish—and also of anguish pure and simple—on the critical faculty of man, and on the spontaneous impulses without which no revolution is possible. Anguish had certainly a primary role in the psychology of 1940–1941. And, so far as England is

---

111 Allied and Axis commanders respectively.
112 Harold Orlansky, Book Review, "The Journey Home", by Mass Observation, *politics*, December 1944. NB Mass Observation was an organisation devoted to sociological observation.

concerned, one should probably admit that at no moment did the British really despair either of their fatherland or of their old institutions, and not even of their ruling class. The whole history of England makes it impossible to think of something like Blanqui's attempt—on October 31, 1870—to eject the inane Trochu[113] and install a Committee of Public Safety. The British, if they had really lost confidence in Churchill, would have called on Stafford Cripps.[114] And if capitalism had been replaced by something, it would certainly not have been by socialism, but rather by the "third alternative". Which "third alternative", in its turn, and whatever people might say to the contrary, is vigorously rooted in the War Communism of Lenin and Trotzky. The British people, and possibly even the wretched lib-labs[115], must be given some credit for not having pushed things so far as a totalitarian dictatorship.

But what we can certainly and unconditionally reproach the lib-labs for is the miserable inertia they are showing now, when confronted with the question of peace.

The situation is immeasurably worse than in 1919. Compared to the Big Three, Lloyd George, Clemenceau and Wilson[116] appear as angels of peace and wisdom. This time, the continent of Europe has been swept by something that could have become a popular revolution. This time, instead of the chauvinistic Parliament hand-picked by Lloyd George, Britain has given power to the Laborites. After the defeat of Hitler, revolutionary defeatism would have been possible, without any danger of playing into the hands of the Nazis. But the impotence of the parties, and the inert disillusionment of the peoples, are today greater than ever.

---

113 Auguste Blanqui (1805–1881), 19th century French republican, socialist and revolutionary activist. Louis-Jules Trochu (1815–1896), head of the French Government of National Defense from September 1870 to February 1871.

114 Stafford Cripps (1889–1952), British Labour Party politician.

115 Lib-labs was the term used by Macdonald and other writers on *politics* for Social Democrats. It derives from the use of the term in British politics for Liberal MPs sponsored by Trades Union branches prior to (and for a short time after) the formation of the Labour Party.

116 David Lloyd-George (1863–1945), Georges Clemenceau (1841–1929), and Woodrow Wilson (1856–1924): the leaders of the UK, France and the USA respectively at the end of the First World War, and hence the key 'Allied' figures in the treaties that ended that war.

Notes on Mass Culture[117]

I. "The Breadline and the Movies," by Melvin J. Lasky[118]*; Politics, 1944.*

1.

Before Augustus' institution of the principate, every candidate to a high office had to contribute out of his own pocket to the expenses for the circus and for the distributions of bread. Once all the offices were monopolised by the emperor, the whole electoral body became automatically the client of the Caesars. In Constantinople, the districts formed by the Hippodrome fans were still not without political influence, and the *basilei*[119] were careful not to displease those people in order not to jeopardize the stability of the throne.

One is reminded of this kind of electoral deal when observing the attention paid by certain Socialist city councils of Southern France to the construction of luxurious stadiums, while the sewage system is majestically neglected. And right now, in France, an intense competition is going on between Communists, Catholics and Socialists, for the organisation of as many sports rallies as possible.

2.

It is evident that the powers-that-be become concerned about not letting the poor starve only when these are gathered in considerable numbers in the proximity of the rich. It is the common custom of Empires to let millions of peasants die of starvation as a result of droughts, floods, or of those peculiar acts of God that are commonly called "historical necessities," like Five Year Plans and such. But Napoleon used to say that

---

117 Article published in *politics* magazine, November 1946. A rather longer version of this essay was included—with the title "People, Mass and Culture"— in A. Caffi, *Critique of Violence,* Indianapolis, Bobbs-Merrill, 1970, a collection of essays that was itself a translation of an Italian collection published in 1966, *Critica della Violenza.*
118 Melvin J Lasky, "The Breadline and the Movies", *politics*, February 1944. For Lasky see note 27 above, and also see Michael Wreszin, *A Rebel in Defence of Tradition, the Life and Politics of Dwight Macdonald*, New York for the Lasky-Macdonald relationship.
119 Basilei is a Greek word that means "kings".

he felt less threatened by the defeat of one of his armies than by Paris being left without bread for two days. From Swift's times[120] to the terrible famine of 1847, no British government ever bothered with anything like a dole in order to prevent millions of Irishmen from starving. And the very synthetic political device of King Bomba[121] of Naples: "*Feste, Farina, Forca*" (Feasts, Flour and Gallows) did not apply to the far-away peasants of Basilicata[122], who could placidly be left to live like animals, but to Naples' *Lazzaroni* [123], whose moods might have for some effect on the security of the regime.

3.

All this reminds us that "ochlocracy"—the rule of the mob—is nearly always the inevitable complement of "plutocracy." The crude shows of the Circus were certainly meant for a mob. But Dyonisos' theatre was in harmony with the esthetic and ethical sensibility of a *demos*. And the Olympic Games, where Herodotus read his Histories, Pindar[124] sung his Odes, and the best sculptors of Greece erected their statues, were an expression of the aristocratic level attained by Athenian democracy. But the professional athletes of the Hellenistic and Roman periods exhibited themselves for the plutocrats and the mob. On the other hand, from Shakespeare and Lope de Vega[125] to the romantic melodrama, modern theatre has certainly contributed to the formation of popular elites. Shall we say that today the movies are meant for the mob? Or maybe it is the radio? Or industrialized sport? Or all of them together?

Something else might be involved, in all this. Namely, the fact that, from the industrial and bureaucratic managers to the humblest worker in a factory, from the pilot of a dive-bomber to the ordinary civilian whose

---

120 Jonathan Swift (1667–1745), Irish writer and satirist best known for writing *Gulliver's Travels* (1726). His satirical essay "A Modest Proposal" (1729) criticized British policies that led to widespread starvation in Ireland.
121 Ferdinand II, King of the Two Sicilies (1810–1859), known as 'King Bomba' for his ordering the naval bombardment of Messina in 1848.
122 A southern province of Italy.
123 The poorest of Naples' lower classes in the revolutionary period. Initially pro-Bourbon by 1860 they had shifted to supporting Garibaldi.
124 Herodotus (c. 484–c. 425 BCE), Greek historian and geographer. Pindar (c. 518–c. 438 BCE), Greek poet.
125 Lope de Vega (1562–1635), Spanish playwright.

frail body has become the natural target of cosmic explosives, modern man is physiologically condemned to spiritual torpor. He has no use for thinking, since thinking can be of no use to him. After a day of work in a modern city, no energy is left for the efforts of the imagination or for any active emotional life. Artistic receptivity, meditation, and the serene contemplation of motionless forms, are equally impossible. While the movies feed their audience with ready-made and suitably fleeting images.

4.

For the last twenty years, precisely this relationship between "ochlocracy", plutocracy, and the totalitarian State, has been the stumbling block of Marxist criticism. Marxism has vainly attempted to explain the evolution of "liberal" capitalism toward State capitalism, and the deviation of the "general will" of the masses toward authoritarian States. This is the problem of the "third alternative" which Dwight Macdonald has rightly affirmed to exist between capitalism and a Socialist organisation of society. It is also the problem of the "New Class Society" so conscientiously analyzed by Peter Meyer in POLITICS. The discussion with W.P. Taylor (December, 1944)[126] shows to what extent this unexpected complication of the traditional views is met by "progressive democrats" with little more than an indignant refusal to understand.

Be it empirically identified with the trusts, the "economic royalists," the 200 families (or the 2,000, as in ancient Rome), or the "upper ten thousand," plutocracy does not seem difficult to define. One should add that the addition of "kratos" to "plutos" sounds rather superfluous. The wealthiest have always been the strongest. This was true of the high priests of Ammon[127], who owned thousands of serfs and millions of acres of Egypt's land; of the Church under Innocent III[128], fat with benefices and tithes; of the Persian satraps; of the Chinese warlords; of the Thessalian landowners; of the French feudal lords whom Joinville calls "les riches hommes"; of the shipbuilders and merchants who ruled Corinth and Venice; etc.

---

126 See: Peter Meyer, "Mr. Joseph Stalin's Revolution in Economic Science", *politics*, June 1944; and W.P. Taylor, "So What?", *politics*, December 1944.
127 The high priests of Ammon (or Amun) were the highest-ranking priests of the ancient Egyptian god Amun.
128 Pope from 1198–1216.

But for a regime to be correctly defined a plutocracy, certain conditions must be fulfilled: first of all, accumulated money ("odorless money," as the French have called it) must have the power to buy anything, from land to offices, from the treasures of Golconda[129] to men's consciences and honor. The obsession with money and its power in the Elizabethan drama, and already in the Greek lyrics of the Sixth century B.C., expresses well the shock caused by such a fact, when it still appears as a novelty.

The second condition is the diffusion, throughout the social structure, of a rationalistic attitude undermining and unmasking as pretense all the values on which the prestige of royalty, priesthood, birth, and of respectability itself, was supposed to be based.

But, above all, the accumulation and use of wealth must have openly taken the form of shameless pillaging, of what the Germans call precisely *Raubbau*—robbers' economy—with its accompaniment of usury on the greatest scale; plunder of the colonies and of the conquered countries; armaments and war; and the exploitation of the fiscal apparatus for personal enrichment.

Such was the situation in Rome during the last two centuries of the Republic; and such is also the form taken by modern capitalism in its "imperialistic phase," and specially after 1920.

As for the "ochlos," it is of course, the very opposite of what we mean by "the people": it is the people uprooted from its communities, oblivious of its "mores," with nothing left of its original mythology but a few but a few discolored shreds of superstition.

The ancient "ochlos" was made up of peasants chased out of their ancestral strips of land; of all the human rubbish which kept on swarming in the ports of the Middle East; and also of the masses of slaves scrambled together and dispersed—as when, in Delos, ten thousand heads of human cattle were being auctioned off in a single day.

As for the modern "ochlos," only a section of it—and not the most important—can be made to correspond to what the Marxists call

---

129 Goldconda is a ruined city on the outskirts of Hyderabad, India, that was
    known for its large diamonds.

Lumpenproletariat. To describe the most numerous, and most significant, component of the modern "ochlos," Marxism has not been able to find a better term than the very elastic, and by now completely worn out one, of "petty-bourgeoisie."

On this point, also, as on many others, we are badly in need of some more detailed analysis.

II. "A Theory of Popular Culture," by Dwight Macdonald; Politics, February, 1944.[130]

Dwight Macdonald distinguishes: 1) a High Culture, which he tends to identify with the products of the avant-garde; 2) a "Popular Culture for the elite," which seems to correspond to academicism; 3) a "Folk Art" which is supposed to be "the common people's own institution"—and it is significant that in this connection only Art is mentioned, disregarding the other aspects of culture: philosophy, scientific notions, moral norms, forms and rites of sociability; 4) finally, Popular Culture for the Masses, which is considered to be: a) fairly debased; b) "an instrument of social domination," but a form of culture nevertheless, i.e., a form of the education of sensibility and intelligence.

May I suggest that a few essential factors are here neglected?

1.

The *people* and the *masses* are two entirely different realities. Georges Gurvitch[131] has rightly pointed out that the *mass* is a form of human relationships which, to start with, has nothing to do with the number of individuals involved. The mass is a way of completely disregarding the

---

130 Dwight Macdonald, "A Theory of Popular Culture", *politics*, February 1944. Macdonald's article and Caffi's critique are mentioned by T. S. Eliot in the 1948 preface to his *Notes towards the Definition of Culture*, London, Faber, 1962 (originally 1948). Eliot apparently met Macdonald at his flat in New York in 1947. See M. Wreszin, *A Rebel in Defense of Tradition*, p. 521 (Footnote 2). Macdonald's essay can be seen as a starting point for a series of works -essays and books- on culture that he produced in the post-World War II period.

131 This is likely a reference to Gurvitch's "Mass, Community, Communion", in *The Journal of Philosophy*, 1941, Vol. 38, No. 18. This draws upon pre-war French language material by Gurvitch which Caffi would likely have been familiar with.

personality of the other fellow by simply adjusting oneself mechanically to his external movements. It involves a form of sociability which is at the same time primitive and inhuman, insofar as critical consciousness, choice, and plurality of spontaneous social relations, are definitely absent from it.

The *people*, on the other hand, necessarily implies the existence of a permanent community, and the possibility of communion in the realization of higher values than those derived from mere utilitarian expediency.

2.

In itself, and for itself, and insofar as exploiters and demagogues have a vested interest in its existence, the *mass* cannot have any culture, if we agree that culture implies a certain activity, a certain free choice, on the part of the individual who "cultivates himself" or agrees to "be cultivated." Mass can only receive psychological shocks (to which it usually reacts by collective hysteria) or imperative suggestions whose results are panic, the automatism of the soldier, the oblivious and hopeless resignation of the beast of burden.

3.

Prussian or fascist drill is the very opposite of education. And the astute thwarting of a human soul by Jesuit or Calvinist pedagogy is also nothing but the perversion of what we ordinarily mean by culture or education.

Hence, there is such a thing in society as the possibility of an "anti-culture," as well as of a sheer lack of culture. The Eskimos possess a culture. But all we know of the wretched Fijians seems to indicate the absence among them of any possibility of a lively esthetic or religious life. On the other hand, the SS and the gaolers of Auschwitz and Dachau had certainly been radically immunised against any germ of culture.

4.

In England, the industrial revolution began around 1750. Engels and Melville[132] observed its effects between 1840–1850. Having been for two

---

132 Possibly a reference to Herman Melville, who was in Britain 1849–1850.

or three generations completely deprived of any contact with the realities from which culture can originate or be kept alive, the men and women of that period had lost all memory of a folk art, and of any real communal life.

The phenomenon has followed industrial capitalism throughout the world: Germany, Poland, Russia, China, etc. Cities like Paris and Lyons seem to have resisted better than others. There, in the nineteenth century, a true popular culture could be found. But what we know of conditions in Alsace, Nantes, the region Lille-Roubaix from 1830 to 1860, tells us the same atrocious tale as Great Britain.

On the other hand, we should remember the level of individual *and* social education among the immigrants who swarmed into America in the nineteenth century from Ireland, Andalusia, Southern Italy, Eastern Europe after having shrivelled for several generations in their ghettos and villages, crushed by unimaginable misery. To them, the liberated Negro slaves should be added, and the natives in the colonies brutalized by bad alcohol and forced labor—or those miserable Moroccans expelled from their fields and reduced to an existence that could not be called life any more.

All these creatures had simply been stripped of everything human. There was no Folk Culture left to repress or corrupt in them, in order to make room for the Ersatz of culture (or the systemic non-culture) thrown on the market by capitalism together with the other articles of current consumption.

The human plant is a sturdy one. The worst slums were somewhat cleared and, through revolts and strikes, the wage-workers wrested a little leisure, some hygiene, a few schools. Then the joy of life, and even physical beauty, started blossoming again. But the past evil could not be abolished. The tastes, desires, dreams, aspirations, myths of those *uprooted* people were not nurtured either by undimmed traditions or by those well-formed and clearly defined qualities and peculiarities whose pattern we call "nature." All the things and all the values made available to them for use or knowledge were not only pre-fabricated but also mass-fabricated.

5.

Who fabricated those things and values? Can we say that the vulgarization of culture in modern times reveals the plan of a "bourgeois ideocracy" which can be compared to the plan applied by the Catholic Church, or to the far more brutal ones carried out by totalitarian states?

The rather startling fact is that the class which seized power in France under Louis-Philippe, and, by a slower process, ended up by occupying in England the places which had in earlier times been monopolized by the gentry, this class never possessed a culture which really reflected its inner convictions and spontaneous preferences. These upstarts simply took over (not without a feeling of uneasiness) the furniture of their predecessors, without ever quite succeeding in making themselves at home. They accepted the humanities; scientific progress; such notions as politeness and luxury; such established values as honor (chivalry), glory (especially military glory), virtue (with a preference for a certain asceticism). But their management of this patrimony was a clumsy affair. They could never get rid of a certain peculiarly suspicious attitude toward such people as artists, scientists and ideologists. Culture has often existed *against them* (even Adam Smith expresses contempt for merchants, specialists, etc.), and they have been scandalized or angered by original creations more often than they have felt proud for having helped them financially.

Parallel with this development, the aristocracy progressively lost its ancient hold on culture and the higher forms of sociability. If compared to the brilliant nobility of the 1820's, with its liberal princes and counts, among whom Pushkin was received as an equal, Nicholas II's courtiers (be they friends or adversaries of Rasputin) were nothing but lamentable idiots. Around Franz Joseph I, during the last part of his reign, one would have looked in vain for such authentically cultivated personages as a Kaunitz, a Metternich, or even a von Gentz.[133] Among the Junkers[134] who enjoyed the favor of Wilhelm II, was there a single one who could be

---

133 Leading figures in the governments of the Habsburg Empire in the 18th and 19th centuries.

134 Junkers were Prussian aristocratic landowners and they dominated the officer corps of the military.

compared to the von Steins, von Hardenbergs, Yorks[135], conversant with Hegel's philosophy and Goethe's[136] poetry?

The peculiar uneasiness, but also the peculiar vigor, of the nineteenth century were due precisely to this fact, that "high culture" found itself shut off both from the ruling classes and from the people. While the people, on the other hand, was itself disappearing into the "mass." Hence, spiritual life was often divorced from the social.

6.

These are some of the reasons why I would venture to suggest the following distinctions:

(A) A Folk Culture which is the spontaneous creation of every popular milieu, and is easily led into sectionalism and regionalism. This Folk Culture is partly leveled by capitalism and the uniformity which is the inevitable counterpart of modern cosmopolitanism, and partly taken over and made sophisticated by high culture (as it has happened with all kinds of folk-traditions in the music, plastic arts and literature of the late nineteenth and the twentieth centuries).

(B) High culture has always been the privilege of an elite. In the past, this elite coincided with a section of the aristocracy and of the clergy. With the formation of the bourgeoisie and with the decay of the churches, the intellectual elite found itself in the ambiguous position of an aristocratic outcast, of non-consecrated clerics, of rebels who escaped spiritually from a social system to which they had to submit in all practical matters.

(C) The several varieties of half-culture, characterized by a lesser or greater amount of conformism, moral inertia, existence without individuality or problems, and especially without any living communion with one's fellow man. This Ersatz-culture is the refuge (and the rampart) of the rulers and managers of the present society, together with their satellites. It is the reign of uneasy conscience and bad taste; of hasty and

---

135 Leading political and military figures in Prussia around the turn of the 18th and 19th centuries. Note: Caffi's 'von Stein' is actually vom Stein, and Caffi's 'York' is actually Yorck von Wartenburg

136 Georg Wilhelm Friedrich Hegel (1770–1831), German philosopher. An important figure for Marx and other German thinkers of the 19th century. Johann Wolfgang von Goethe (1749–1832), influential German polymath.

unscrupulous work; of insincerity in all its forms; of artifice and "kitsch"; of official optimism and solemn boredom; of what Flaubert[137] called *pignouflisme.*

(D) Aggressive and destructive Anti-Culture. It represents a tremendous force, a motorized barbarianism a thousand times more devastating than Tamburlan's cavalry.[138] It has at its command all the resources of "applied science" together with the possibility of exploiting *rationally* the lowest instincts of the human animal.

Aggressive Anti-Culture can count among its most recent achievements: 1) modern militarism forced on everybody without distinction, and now perfected according to its inner logic by the atom bomb; 2) the extermination of several colonial peoples (where the naive barbarianism of the Spaniards had failed; 3) the totalitarian state of Hitler and Stalin—which, for all we know, might not be the last word in this field; 4) modern propaganda, based on the degradation of all intellectual and emotional values, and consequently of all human dignity and authenticity in things spiritual.

(E) As for the masses, as long as they remain masses (in the sense I have indicated), there is no possibility of culture. To feed them party slogans, to gather them into a circus of some kind, to talk to them through loudspeakers, means to order them around, not to cultivate them.

On the other hand, the new popular communities who succeed in extricating themselves from the masses have several ways of cultivating themselves, however hazardous. In the past, the labor unions, the cooperatives, certain religious sects, the Socialist Internationals have contributed to this task. But the role of smaller formations, like certain groups of friends among the French workers, should not be underestimated.

What these spontaneous social formations most need is, in order to be put on guard against cultural Ersatz and helped to withstand the onslaught

---

137 Gustave Flaubert (1821–1880), French novelist and leading exponent of literary realism.
138 The 16th century play *Tamburlaine the Great* was loosely based on the life of the Mongol emperor Timur. In the play, Tamburlaine went from humble beginnings to becoming a world-conquering emperor.

of anti-culture, is the guidance of people capable of giving them advice; and, in order to defend their material existence against the pressure of an hostile milieu, a kind of cooperative organisations (*sic*) adapted to the peculiar character of each group.

To encourage the formation of such groups, to educate as many educators as possible, to provide material support for such organisations, should be a very important function of any modern Socialist movement. And one must confess that in the field of actual education, Marxist socialism has failed in a particularly lamentable way. "Class consciousness" was supposed to take care of everything.

EUROPEAN

Violence and Sociability[139]

by "European"

My thesis is that a movement for the achievement of "bread, liberty, peace," the deliverance of society from the coercive apparatus of the State, the ending of competing, hostile "nations," and the abolition of wage-labor and classes—my thesis is that such a movement cannot consider useful, or even possible, the means of organized violence: i.e., (a) armed insurrection, (b) civil war, (c) international war (even if against Hitler—or Stalin), (d) a dictatorial and terroristic regime to consolidate the "new order."

My first argument, based on experience and common sense, is that these means are not effective and seem to lead to the very opposite result from the one aimed at. This argument, a "pragmatic" one, has been developed often enough already, by pacifists and by critics of Bolshevism, and so I shall not go into it here at any length. Instead, I want to develop two other and less familiar lines of argument in favor of a position of principled non-violence: one that looks to the thoughts and feelings which have evolved with striking unanimity ever since man began to reflect on his destiny; the other flowing from the unprecedented situation which contemporary man faces.

●

Disgust with violence is perhaps as old as the use of violence; enthusiasm for violence is without doubt a product of fairly modern "moods" which there are good reasons to consider artificial and morbid. The integral pacifism of the Buddhists would never have succeeded in winning so many adherents if there had not been an intimate correspondence between its precepts and the sentiments of the people. There are signs

---

139 Article published in *politics* magazine, January 1947. A rather longer version of this essay was included in A Caffi, *Critique of Violence*, 1970, under the title "A Critique of Violence". This essay has also been translated into Italian as "Violenza e socievolezza" in the April and May 1958 editions of the anarchist journal *Volontà*, and into German in the April 2017 edition of *Grasswurzel Revolution* as "Eine Kritik der Gewalt".

that during the neolithic age (which may have lasted more than 10,000 years) peace between the settled communities, and within them, was unbroken and complete. Savage invaders armed with bronze, and later with iron, came on the scene to fill the world with carnage and military glory, and spread that drunkenness the most typical frenzies of which are represented by the Kings of Assyria and the Mongol Khans. During the long last century, from the "conscripts of the Year II"[140] to the SS of Hitler, the Stalinist marshals and generals like the late Patton[141], Western man (not to mention Japan and China—"new and warlike") has felt this fever of violence in all its forms: patriotic exaltation, revolutionary romanticism, the "white man's burden," striving towards a point "beyond Good and Evil," Sorelian reflections on violence, the various forms of terror; Jacobin, Bolshevist, Fascist.

Before this tidal wave, pacifism, which seemed to have gained ground in the eighteenth century, has not only given way but, even worse, has yielded to a kind of cowardly imitativeness by seeking a solution (providential or "dialectical") on the very road down which its adversaries have marched from triumph to triumph, and from catastrophe to catastrophe. The rationalistic pacifism of the liberals made too many concessions not only to patriotism, but even to political expediency. The pacifism of Robert Owen, Saint-Simon, and of Proudhon; the evangelism of the Quakers, and later of Leo Tolstoi[142], could be admired by some people, derided by others; but the implication always was that those men were talking some kind of touching nonsense. The kind of hope that was considered reasonable, and was shared by multitudes, found satisfaction in the image of a "final conflict" subsequent to which humanity would find itself united in the International; or in a "war to end all wars"; or, even more mechanically, in the idea that instruments of destruction so terrifying that nobody would dare use them would be devised. The action

---

140 Year II – of the French Revolution.

141 General George Patton (1885–1945), US general in World War II., memorably portrayed by George C. Scott in the 1970 film *Patton*.

142 Robert Owen (1771–1858), Welsh social reformer, co-operator and early socialist thinker. Henri de Saint-Simon (1760–1825), French social theorist and early socialist thinker. Pierre-Joseph Proudhon (1809–1865), French socialist theorist. Leo Tolstoi (1828–1910), Russian novelist and social thinker.

of a man like Jaures[143] in defence of peace was radically undermined by his acceptance of "national sovereignty." The antimilitarism of the French anarchists and syndicalists was made morally weak by the fact that, while condemning war between States, they upheld revolutionary violence in the struggle between classes.

Let us look at the source of the "cultivated" man's aversion to violence.

Condorcet[144] was expressing the opinion of a great number of his "enlightened" contemporaries when he wrote: "As civilization spreads over the globe, war and conquest will disappear, and slavery and misery with them." "Civilization" was a new word in the eighteenth century. It is not to be found in a French book before 1765, and Dr. Johnson[145] still refused to include it in his dictionary. The Scot, Millar[146], in his "Observations on the Beginnings of Society" (French edition, 1773) defined it as "that politeness of *mores* which is the natural consequence of abundance and security." And the French Abbé Girard[147], in 1780, wrote that politeness "adds to simple civility what devotion adds to the exercise of public worship: the means to a human group more affectionate, *more interested in others*, more refined"; which, in its turn, presupposes "a more consistent culture, and certain natural qualities, or the difficult art of stimulating them." From 1736 on, Voltaire stressed the idea that politeness cannot be conceived as "something arbitrary, like what we call civility: it is a law of nature . . . which the French, since the reign of Anne of Austria, have happily cultivated more than other peoples have," becoming, thanks to it, "the *most sociable* people in the world."

---

143 Jean Jaurès (1859–1914), French Socialist leader in the years up to the First World War. He was assassinated 31 July 1914.

144 Nicholas de Condorcet (1743–1794), French philosopher, political economist and politician. Participated in the Revolution but branded a traitor by the convention, he died in prison.

145 Samuel Johnson (1709–1784), English writer, who was commonly referred to as Dr. Johnson, published one of the most influential English dictionaries in history titled *A Dictionary of the English Language* (1755).

146 John Millar (1735–1801), Scottish philosopher and historian.

147 Gabriel Girard (1677–1748), French clergyman and grammarian. His most famous work, *Synonymes français* (1718), appears to have been republished in 1780, which is likely what Caffi was referring to.

And Duclos[148] in 1731 pointed out the difference between primitive peoples, among whom "distinction and nobility are based on *force*" and civilized countries, "where the most highly prized distinction is intellectual."

What is in question here is "mores," "culture," "humanity," and not any metaphysical principle or religious precept. From the Athenian who treated his slave "humanely" to the English lady who reprimanded the cabman who beat his horse, refinement and politeness essentially meant refraining from all violence in behaviour. In the name of what? In the name of "self-respect," which is inconceivable without respect for others. It is sociability, naturally spread from one to another, until it includes all living beings. It is, on the surface, good education, cultivated manners; beneath the surface, intellectual awareness of society, as a fact and as a value—hence, inevitably, of *justice*, conceived as an idea more fundamental than any religious or moral dogma. But sociability and justice do not exist without a desire of happiness for all, without which one could not oneself be happy ("this idea of happiness, so new in Europe," said Saint Just[149], while he was sending people to the scaffold, so as to hasten the realization of the idea). Let us insist: justice implies equality; happiness excludes all oppression; hence an irremediable opposition exists between aspiration to "sociability" and will to power. All violence is by definition antisocial.

But antisocial barbarity exists in us (lust for possession, rancor, natural cruelty, fear, ignorance, etc.) and around us (since civilisation, politeness, cultivated sociability have remained until now the privilege of a minority of people located in a limited number of places). Hence for thousands of years, barbarism—especially barbarism coated with a varnish of "civility"— has triumphed. Over and over again, for the sake of bare survival, men have sacrificed the reasons for living. For centuries, this compromise has been more or less successful, i.e. because of it a number of sincere adversaries of violence have survived, although not without from time to

---

148 Charles Pinot Duclos (1704–1772), French writer who contributed to the *Encyclopedie.*

149 Louis de Saint Just (1767–1794), ally of Maximilien Robespierre in the French Revolution, who was nicknamed "The Archangel of Terror".

time either submitting to violent commandments or using violence themselves. But where are we today?

•

Plato entrusted the defense (*sic*) of his Republic to warriors expressly drilled, "like hounds," for carnage. But he also insisted that his State should never wage aggressive war, since any aggrandizement would have wrecked the harmony of the ideal commonwealth. Moreover, the armed caste is farther from wisdom, the "essential aim" of the Republic, than are the workers. It is a fair guess that, in Plato's State, the sociability and the "mores" of the common people would be as "humanized" as possible, while the warriors would be restricted to sheer inhumanity.

The problem to which Plato's work attempts to give an answer seems to be how to conceive of a society capable of achieving a supreme degree of civilization while at the same time having to protect itself against a barbaric environment. Hence Plato imagines his city: (1) as a lonely island in an ocean of human imperfection, and having only occasional contacts with the external world; (2) as a place where inevitable evil will be granted its share once and for all, by relegating a section of the population to the job of violence, while workers and philosophers will enjoy and cultivate the benefits of peaceful and polite intercourse.

Such a situation, and such a division, are far from being utopian. They have been in fact the conditions under which a number of civilized societies have existed, provided the struggle between the classes did not take a violent form. Which is precisely the danger that Plato believed he had eliminated in his State.

During the eighteenth, and a good part of the nineteenth century, in spite of universal conscription introduced by the French Revolution, violence was an exception, limited in time as well as in space; its practice mostly the business of professional people. And it was generally thought that such a practice would become rarer and rarer, less and less brutal; in a word, that violence could be "humanized." It is only since 1914 that man has come to experience the reign of total violence, violence unlimited, unmeasurable, and practically uninterrupted. What has become of civilization, "mores," politeness, under such a regime, does not have to be described. Whether we believe in some kind of religion—be it the "religion of progress" or the vaguest kind of humanism—or in no religion at all, we are all confronted with the dilemma stated by Dwight Macdonald: either we "get" the machinery of violent coercion which has transformed our lives into one huge fear, or else the machinery will "get" us, and with us the patrimony of culture, politeness, justice, happiness which gives some meaning to our existence.

Can we conquer violence through violence?

This question really conceals two different problems. The first is an empirical one: what probability is there that a group of free men, fully conscious of their aim, will be able to obtain an armament, an equipment, a technical skill that will enable them to fight the present masters of the world with a reasonable chance of success? But the really decisive problem is the second: let's assume that it is possible to launch a mass action powerful enough to fight a serious battle for the possession of the highly technical engines (from the atom bomb to the superpoisons, and from the superpoisons to the structures of economic and political power) that today threaten the very existence of mankind. Can anyone seriously believe in the probability of avoiding, under circumstances as "revolutionary" as you like, a backsliding into, and in fact a dependence on, the habits of savagery, the impulsion of the will to power, the division of all involved in the struggle into docile hordes and imperious leaders? Are we not to expect these realities when we place our reliance on organized violence? And then again, as after Thermidor in France, as in 1918-1919 throughout Europe, as under Stalin in Russia, will it not be permissible to ask: "Why has so much blood been shed? To what idol have these countless young lives been sacrificed?" And is it possible to answer such questions if one does not regard the exercise of force as sacred, and heroic sacrifice as an end in itself?

Who was more devoted than Robespierre and Saint Just, to the cause of the people, to the aim of enabling the people to govern themselves in "liberty, equality and fraternity?" And surely Lenin and Trotsky fought to their last breath for the union of humanity in a socialist federation. But the French leaders were the very ones to dam every spontaneous surge of the people of Paris, demoralizing them by means of the Terror, reducing the Clubs to official meetings attended by frightened bureaucrats. It was Robespierre and Saint Just who centralized and militarized France (which implied the consolidation of a new ruling caste of bureaucrats, generals and great munition-makers) so that the country was ripe for Napoleonic despotism and a bourgeois oligarchy. And, it was the Russian leaders who were responsible for the crushing of the Soviets, the installation of the all-powerful Tcheka, the imposition on the workers of the police regime of State-controlled unions, the multiplication of arbitrary powers, and all sorts of other yokes, economic and political. In short, they prepared the way for the Stalinist autocracy. Neither traitors nor weaklings, the Jacobins and the Bolsheviks achieved these results by the employment of revolutionary terror; and in the exercise of this terror, as well as in the actions that followed from their course, their essentially *antisocial* mentality is revealed to us: *the French Jacobins and the Russian communists saw society exclusively in terms of certain power-relationships; aiming at governmental organization or controlled economy in the name of the people or the proletariat, while considering as mere by-products the manners, sociability, justice, happiness which constitute the immediate content of real existence and real freedom.*

If we examine the whole sequence of revolutions and counter-revolutions since the revolt of the American colonists against the British Crown, the striking uniformity with which certain circumstances are repeated is enlightening (despite the certainly plausible view that history never teaches anybody anything).

Let us agree to call *society* the ensemble of spontaneous and pleasurable relations among men, insofar as there is at least the appearance of freedom in the act of forming or breaking relations with others (no pressure being exerted except through "moral means"), while utilitarian motives are either really sublimated or camouflaged by politeness and the pleasure of being together. This is to say that *society*, taken in this sense, implies the rejection in principle of any kind of constraint and more especially of every form of violence. It should be fairly clear that the strength, the continuity, and even the partial successes (for the forms of oppression can indeed be crushing) of a human movement for emancipation are directly calculable in terms of the level of "social" life. While no armed body increases the chances for success of such a movement, or contributes to any real progress achieved by it.

The thirteen American States were tightly woven "societies" much more than political or military formations. The Puritan culture was no doubt narrow and tyrannical, but it was to the taste of the vast majority. On the other hand, it is owing to the "anarchy" of the *szlachta*—a form of communal life where extreme sociability was allied to a most punctilious sense of personal independence—that the Poles were able to oppose such astounding resistance to powerful oppressors for so long a period in spite [of] the poverty of the country and of the lamentable policy of the national governments. And it is because they were, as Voltaire said, "the most sociable people in the world," that the French have been until 1871 at the head of the European revolutionary movement. As for Russia, the tremendous scale of the October Revolution cannot be understood without taking into account the parallel action, during a century, of the religious sects (which were communistic and, most of them, stubbornly pacifistic) and, on the other hand, of the humanitarian *Intellighentsia*, accompanied by the flowering of "society" in St. Petersbourg, Moscow, etc. The more refined sociability of Vienna as compared to Berlin, and the barrenness of social life in Italy (so bitterly lamented by Leopardi[150]), throw a good deal of light on the vicissitudes of the 1848 revolutions. In Spain, the powerful antisocial forces which dominated the country since the Counter-reformation and Philip II[151] were successfully resisted not by Castilian authoritarianism but by the separatist tendencies developed in Barcelona, and by the forms of anarchist solidarity spread throughout the Peninsula.

●

Marx's resounding dictum, "Violence is the midwife of history," lacks subtlety. The hemorrhages caused by the historical forceps may be more or less serious, the operation itself may be not at all successful. There are the insurrections caused by despair or fanaticism, and drowned in blood; after the hacking of the foetus, the patient—"civilization"—does not always recover. There are the coups d'état which we are accustomed to call "reactionary" insofar as their aim is to stop or to prevent a popular movement; this sort of enterprise is always preceded by organized violence directed at suppressing social spontaneity in order to establish or

---

150 Giacomo Leopardi (1798–1837), Italian poet and essayist of the first half of the 19th century.

151 Philip II (1527–1598), King of Spain and later King of Portugal who sought to be a defender of Catholic Europe against Protestantism and the Ottoman Empire.

reinforce the power of a State, a party, a leader, or an arbitrary "order." And then there are the "revolutions." They are the outcome of a spontaneous agreement between the aspirations nourished for a long time among the people at large, and the ideas developed by smaller groups, the "society." Hence the atmosphere of joy, of radiant hope, of brotherly getting together, which characterizes these "dawns of a new era." The outbursts of violence that mark the triumph of such movements are as sudden as they are short-lived and limited. The storming of the Bastille; July, 1830 in Paris; February and March, 1848, throughout Europe; March, 1917, in Russia; April, 1931, in Spain, were not what we would call bloody battles. With characteristic generosity and humanity, the conquerors have often taken pride in having won freedom without shedding blood.

We know, however, that the dream dreamed during such days can have no future. The first triumph of a popular movement has always been followed by tragedy.

Here two points must be considered.

The first is that the quasi-rationalism born during the Renaissance has not only drained the marshes of superstition; it has also dried up what might be called the "myth-making" side of human nature. Hence, Western man is accustomed to consider institutions, laws, police, everything disciplined and instrumental, as more real, more consistent, more manageable than the spontaneous ways, the unorganized forms of solidarity, the collective mentality, of the social milieu. Hence the barbaric fallacy of considering what is most intimate and vital in man as a by-product of what is most external and crude. Hence the barbaric principle, universally accepted in our days, that what is most delicate and precious in man is also, by definition, what can legitimately be violated and crushed.

Secondly, very few persons are capable of perceiving clearly the evident fact that a revolution is after all only the official consecration of changes (in the distribution of wealth, social and political influence, cultural primacy, etc.) which have already taken place. While, on the other hand, whatever substantial changes still remain to be accomplished (new ways of life, opportunities for new social strata, general "cultivation" of the new forms of social existence) can be realized only gradually, in a period of time extending possibly over several generations. People are at the same time impatient for a total change and eager not to be left for one single day without the apparatus which guarantees the continuity of social order. Hence the disillusionments. Hence the inexperienced hands shaking the social machinery in order to get it started again. Hence also, the preference for a "prompt return to normalcy" over a more farsighted putting up with inconveniences which might well prove healthy in the end. All this is chaotic, and breeds nothing but chaos. Chaos in turn breeds violence.

Of course, there are always, or nearly always, people unafraid of chaos and ready to exploit it. To my knowledge, the American Revolution is quite exceptional in view of the fact that the leadership remained at the helm until the very end. The American Revolution is unique also in that it was an insurrection with limited aims, and with few social complications. No subsequent revolution was so fortunate. The Jacobins managed to frustrate the plans of royalist reaction; after which came Terror. The Bolsheviks were able to destroy Kornilof[152]; after which came tyranny. In 1848, the Bonapartists, after Blanqui's failure and the June repression, had only the weak-kneed leaders of the Mountain[153] to deal with; again, despotism. Gil Robles[154] first, and Franco after, held cards which neither the FAI[155] nor Negrin[156] could match; once more tyranny. Here we have the third moment of "revolution:" the victory of dictatorial violence addressed either to the "perpetuation" of the conquests of the people, or to the restoration of a more or less mythical "old regime." But in both cases the organs of coercion are strengthened at the expense of "society" and civilization.

Naturally, the supporters of revolutionary violence were always hoping to "do better next time." Today, however, it might well be fatal to engage forces using techniques like those employed during the last six years of total war. And what if once again the enterprise miscarries—as has always happened? And what if in the end we are forced to submit to a

---

152 Lavr Kornilof (1870–1918), more commonly spelled Kornilov, Russian military officer who led a failed military coup d'état in September 1917.
153 Called 'Montagnards' in French.
154 José María Gil-Robles y Quiñones (1898–1980), Spanish rightist politician in the period before the Civil War.
155 FAI — Iberian Anarchist Federation.
156 Juan Negrín (1892–1956), Spanish socialist politician, and Republican premier of Spain when the Republic lost to Franco's forces.

monstrously strengthened apparatus of domination, which we cannot pretend would not be equipped with the atom bomb? Evidently, we must seek for means that are more certain, and more congruent with our aims. And, since we said that the present situation is historically unprecedented, surely we are justified in calling for the invention of strategies and tactics never yet resorted to, and of which only suggestions can be found in what has already been experienced.

●

So then, to the question: "On what principles can one base a struggle against the status quo which would not bring into play organized violence of any sort?" My answer is (A) violence is incompatible with the values of civilisation, of the sociable humanity which we want to save from destruction. In employing violence, we will ourselves be forced to deny the very values we are upholding. (B) The mechanical resources, and massive systems of organization (armies and police forces; Cheka or Gestapo; Dachau, Auschwitz, Siberian camps; Nazi regimes in occupied countries, Russian regime in Poland, etc.), that are now utilized in the violent struggle between human groups, have reached such a degree of horrible efficiency that the complete destruction of civilized society, if not humanity itself, is no longer an idle fancy.

●

What about the "socialist" parties?

In a recently published book, a French factory worker, Georges Navel[157], tells the story of his life. "When I was fifteen," he says, "I was fed up with the workshop and its discipline. I wanted then and there a more noble, more dignified life, a life in which I would not be a worker any longer, in a country where there would be nothing but space, and no industry." Despair became so overpowering that one day this adolescent jumped over the parapet of a bridge into the Rhone River. All he got was a dirty bath, after which he went back to his conveyor belt. All his subsequent attempts to get away from his misery, or to "have a life *outside* the factory"

---

157 Georges Navel (1904–1993), French writer, laborer, and anarchist. The book in reference is likely *Travaux* (1945), which was translated into English in 1949 as *Man at Work*.

ended in failure. "Eight hours in a factory exhausts a man's energy. What he gives to work is not only his time but his life, the very flower of his energy. Even if his particular tasks are not miserably boring and exhausting, at the end of the day he is worn out, sick, his imagination completely dulled . . . In the morning, I didn't wake up until I was shaken by the din of the factory, which followed me everywhere after work. I had become for all eternity a bit of the factory." On the last page of his book, Georges Navel has this to say: "There is a sadness of the worker which cannot be healed by anything but except political action."

Socialists and communists are enchanted by such a conclusion. To them, it shows the right degree of "proletarian consciousness." As for myself, I cannot help but notice that for a worker to participate in a mass movement in no way implies that he has found a way of fulfilling his life. Fulfillment (*sic*) must be distinguished from a resentment that has found a way to be effective, and so must happiness from the rational clarification of despair. For a man of such sincerity, tried by such suffering, political action cannot be a real answer. Such business as party organisation, mass meetings and parades, propaganda slogans, electoral campaigns, or even conspiracies and armed insurrections, can be to him only an Ersatz for what he really needs. This might, among other things, explain the heart-rending disproportion between the sublime sacrifices of the rank and file and the results that the leaders seek (or are able) to achieve.

Here, politics clearly appears as a substitute—often a derisive one—for the social, i.e. whatever substantial content might be found in such notions as civilization, human dignity, equality and fraternity, as well as in the ideal of a spontaneous communion between men fully conscious of their human fate.

From its most remote beginnings, in the ideas of the great thinkers and in the feelings of oppressed peoples, the trend which we today call "socialism" has meant nothing if not a special concern with the reality of human relations based on spontaneity, friendliness, politeness, equality. Institutions, governmental activities, factional struggles (which contain—and often stifle—society) have always been considered by true socialists either malignant tumors to be extirpated altogether, or else a set of inevitable evils to be relentlessly restrained and circumscribed.

If Plato was led to conceive of a city where "all would be held in common," it was because of his disgust with politics, not only with the tyrannical politics of the Thirty[158], but also with that of their "democratic" successors, who put Socrates to death. But another motive also inspired *The Republic*: despair about the fate of that Hellenic civilization which Plato was trying to find a way to preserve. After the ravages of the Peloponnesian Wars and the terroristic regime established in Athens by Critias and his colleagues, the city was visibly going to pieces: social customs, political institutions and spiritual life were disintegrating; private interests were irreconcilable with public welfare; philosophical speculation was losing contact with popular beliefs. So that finally, in a famous passage in one of his letters, Plato reaches the conclusion that, for the time being, there is no solution; one can only wait for some unpredictable turn of the historical tide. But can one do anything, while waiting? Nobody can be sure whether or not Plato seriously believed that, in the expectation of better (or worse) times, one could preserve the quintessence of Hellenic civilization by the creation of small "model cities" inspired by philosophical wisdom, much in the same way as the monasteries would later preserve ancient culture. Perhaps the philosopher was aware that the nostalgic yearning for a more human society would be kept alive only through the influence exercised by the monuments of Greek culture on sects, cenacles, schools, and, possibly, popular movements. In any case, Plato's example seems to suggest that there are moments in history when it is reasonable and farsighted to give up hope in any kind of immediate, large-scale results.

As for the other representatives of the socialist tradition, surely, even before getting a first-hand knowledge of the business of politics as Chancellor of England, Thomas More put little trust in the governments of his time. He thought of his Island of Utopia as a garden where the faculties of the sociable and peaceful individual would not be interfered with in any way by the hands of authority. Thomas Campanella had the vision of his "City of the Sun" only after the failure of his Calabrian plot, and the imprisonment that followed it, had forced him out of politics. Both More and Campanella[159] put their ideal societies under governments

---

158 The Thirty Tyrants (404–403 BCE) were a tyrannical oligarchy that were imposed by the Spartans on Athens during the Peloponnesian War.
159 Authors of early utopias.

patterned after the classical model. In the seventeenth and eighteenth centuries (as under the Hellenistic monarchies), many reformers were hopeful enough to believe that some "enlightened despot" might protect the flowering of ideal communities. On the other hand, in the Middle Ages, representatives of messianic communism like the Italian Fra Dolcino[160] or the Moravian Brothers[161] took their models from the free cities and the "cantons" of liberated peasants. As for the Quakers and the Anabaptists, they never paid much attention to institutional questions.

In all these cases, the means might be discussed, but the aim is clearly a more human *society*. And the attainment of such an aim is thought to be possible only *outside of* the framework of existing institutions.

In modern times, Saint-Simon's first work (*Letters of an Inhabitant of Geneva*) denounces the mistake of the Revolution in having tried to apply a political remedy to a disorder that was essentially social. Robert Owen did not take any part either in the radical ferment of 1820 or, later, in the Chartist agitation. Proudhon, while going to the barricades in February, 1848, did not believe that the people could obtain any benefit from a political revolution, and considered it futile to "organize the Republic" when the real problem was the "organization of society." Saint-Simon, Robert Owen, and eventually also Proudhon, considered that a truly "liberal" regime would have furnished a fairly good opportunity for their plans of social reorganization. The stress was always on *society*, never on institutions.

On the other hand, Babeuf, Blanqui, Louis Blanc[162], and, without any doubt, Karl Marx, saw in the Committee of Public Safety a successful first draft of that dictatorship of the proletariat which would ensure the triumph of socialism. Nobody can say that such means have not been most thoroughly tried.

A last hope remains: the alloy socialism-democracy. It was the ponderous creation of the Second International. What was meant by "democracy"

---

160 13th and 14th century leader of a heretical movement initially called Apostolics, and then Dulcinians.
161 Still extant proto-protestant Church founded in Moravia 60 years before Luther split the Catholic Church.
162 Gracchus Babeuf (1760–1797), French communist. Louis Blanc (1811–1882), French socialist.

was a strongly centralized administration, formidably armed, supported by a large budget, and animated by the "national spirit." This machinery was under the surveillance of the "representatives of the people." "Public opinion" (identified with the people) had the possibility, nay, the duty, of controlling it, thanks to the complete freedom of the press as well as of assembly; and to the competition between parties. All this of course depended on the hypothesis that the complexity of the machinery itself, and the allowance to be made for the highly specialized functions of civil and military "experts," would not make of democratic control a sheer illusion. In any case, socialism was shrewdly to exploit this powerful means, and eventually scrap what was bad in it, preserving what was good.

What happened to this most cumbersome of all Utopias is ancient history already. Because of their rapid successes among the masses, the socialist parties shifted soon from intransigence to reform, and from reform to effective collaboration with the "bourgeois State." Reform gave the workers many material advantages. But reform, and collaboration, inevitably also meant more power, more resources, more bureaucracy for the State. Not to speak of nationalism. The socialist parties engaged all their forces in "democratic" action. Socialism (i.e., the creation of real communities, the civilization of habits, actual justice in actual society) got only rhetoric. The real talk was about the socialist State, or State socialism. In 1914, the powerful fiction of "social-democracy" collapsed.

Now, in 1914 precisely, the great modern "democracies" took the first steps down the road that leads to the *totalitarian State*, i.e., the *total* suppression of society. The point we have reached today is best exemplified by what happened at Oak Ridge[163], U.S.A. POLITICS has rightly stressed the ominous significance of the fact that, in the country which seemed the least affected by State omnipotence, it has been possible to employ for over a year 120,000 workers without their having *the faintest idea of what they were making.* And what they were making was a missile able to kill 300,000 people in a few minutes. Yesterday, it was done to "avenge Pearl Harbor." Tomorrow it will be done to

---

163 Oak Ridge, Tennessee, home to an important plant—which is what Caffi is alluding to here—connected to the production of the Atomic Bombs used in World War II.

obliterate some dangerous example of "anarchy." At this point, democracy clearly needs some mending.

As for social-democracy, the bottom has been officially reached with Leon Blum's[164] declaring, not without coquetry: "I am a Frenchman first, and after that a socialist."

Frankly, it seems to me that the idea of mass action with the slogan "Workers of the World Unite" and the grandiose aim of the "leap from the reign of necessity into the reign of freedom," has worn itself out completely. Where could we summon the courage to start it all over again, from the strictly organized small group to the great and well disciplined mass parties; from the mass parties to the Fourth, or Fifth, International; and from there, where to?

What is left?

A few scattered individuals, and groups, that might find in a resolute pessimism about the immediate future the courage not to despair of the "eternal good cause" of man.

Marx and Engels have written, and Messrs Thorez and Togliatti[165] are now repeating with devotion, that socialism is identical with humanism. I am afraid that the fathers of scientific socialism were thinking especially of such things as philosophy and philology, which were being so successfully cultivated in German Universities. Together with science in general, philosophy and philology would enlighten the proletarian, and help him become fully conscious of his historical mission.

But what was most important in the movement called "humanism" was neither the Renaissance of letters and of the arts, nor the "humanities," which, as the Jesuits showed, could well be used to enslave the human mind to conformism and falsehood. From the sixteenth to the nineteenth centuries, the most important manifestation of humanism was the development of a *free sociability*. This meant, first and foremost, that men started choosing their associates freely, above and beyond all barriers

164 Léon Blum (1872–1950), French Socialist leader, and Prime Minister of France three times, twice before and once after World War II. Imprisoned in the Buchenwald concentration camp, 1943-45.
165 Leaders of the French and Italian Communist Parties respectively at the time this article appeared.

of caste, nationality, or religion. Hence, relations based on true politeness, i.e. on equality and mutual trust, replaced the ceremonious and suspicious artifices of "hierarchical respect."

Today, the multiplication of groups of friends, sharing the same anxieties and united by respect for the same values, would have more importance than a huge propaganda machine. Such groups would not need any compulsory rule. They would not rely on collective action, but rather on personal initiative and effective solidarity, such as can be developed only by friends who know each other well.

Christianity made its most astounding conquests when it was divided in a number of autonomous Churches, connected with each other by "communion" in the same faith, but without any well defined hierarchy or "oecumenic" authority of synods or patriarchs. In the eighteenth century, the cenacles of *libertins* and "encyclopaedists"; the small "societies of atheists" to which references can be found in Fielding and Smollett[166]; the masonic lodges and the *salons* where "people conversed," developed an irresistible propaganda, and established contacts between men from one end of Europe to the other. Those people did not need any central organization which would make decisions and issue sanctions in their name. But, because they aimed at changing attitudes rather than things, society rather than institutions, they certainly caused some real change in this world.

(Translated by Nicola Chiarmonte.)

---

166 Henry Fielding (1707–1754), English author, notably of *The History of Tom Jones* (1749). Tobias Smollett (1721–1771), Scottish writer, notably of *The Adventures of Roderick Random* (1748).

The French Condition[167]

To understand the France of today, we must look back to 1914. The situation cannot be explained solely in terms of defeat, occupation, and the exhaustion following a struggle conducted under particularly trying circumstances: devastation of the country by the "liberators" as well as the enemy, equivocal nature of the Resistance, squandering of human lives according to notions of "national greatness" and "mass action," i.e., the values of DeGaulle and of the Communists respectively. Rather, today there are coming to light all the losses of vitality, all the corruption, bankruptcy and socio-political decay which already existed in the 1918–1939 period and which were not remedied while there was perhaps yet time.

1. French Militarism

For many generations, the majority of Frenchmen were willing to pay the cost of that idea of national greatness (*"grandeur"*) which the Revolution and Napoleon had assimilated to the idea of patriotism. Proposals by bourgeois statesman under Louis Philippe[168] and after 1870 were definitely unpopular. So, too, the anti-militarism of Saint-Simon, Proudhon and the syndicalists was restricted to a rather small circle of intellectuals; in the revolutionary *avant-garde* itself the most generous professions of pacifism and internationalism were mixed with a leaning toward the Strong State (*"Republique une et indivisible"*) and a "people's army" when "the fatherland is in danger"; Jaurès is a good example. From time to time, of course, the Augean stables[169] of militarism had to be cleaned out lest they infect the Republic (Boulanger, the Dreyfus case[170]).

---

167 Article published in *politics*, July–August 1947. Note: this was a special issue on "French Political Writing", with articles by Camus, Simone de Beauvoir, Georges Bataille, Jean-Paul Sartre, and Maurice Merleau-Ponty *inter-alia*.

168 Louis Philippe I (1773–1850), King of France 1830–1848.

169 In Greek mythology, King Augeas owned a vast number of cattle and their stables had not been cleaned for many years and there was an overwhelming amount of filth, which Hercules was tasked with cleaning.

170 Georges Ernest Boulanger (1837–1891), French politician and Minister of War, 1886–1887. In the late 1880s, he was head of the "Boulangist" political

The French general staff maintained its "honor" in World War I even though technically it was not prepared, and the people produced millions of docile soldiers resigned to the most unbelievable sacrifices.

The only rational outcome of that war would have been a new organization of Europe which would have permitted a general disarming. As we know, the very opposite took place, and each nation fell into the absurdity of trying to find a security based on force without the possibility of ever gathering really effective force. Hence it was impossible after 1918 to do away with a French general staff, aureoled with victory, which was also indispensable for the occupation of the Rhine, of Syria, etc. But among the common people, without its ever crystallizing into a new consciousness of international fraternity, a vague feeling spread that "to begin all that again" would be simply suicidal; while among the upper classes the conviction that "war doesn't pay"—i.e., does not buttress the dominant position of the rich—was mixed with dreams of a Praetorian Guard to keep order internally. Colonial warfare came to a standstill: episodes like the campaign against Abd El Krim[171] cannot be compared to the conquests of North Africa, Indochina and Madagascar between 1880 and 1910. The army rested on its laurels and limited itself to preparing to fight another 1914 war, correcting the mistakes made then.

In short, it was a completely decadent military system which Daladier brought into action in 1939, with the ineffable Gamelin[172] at its head. After the debacle, DeGaulle, the obstinate visionary, wanted to bring it back to life, motorized. But the people did not respond; the Resistance militia—

---

movement. The Dreyfus case was a famous case centring on the wrongful conviction of Captain Alfred Dreyfus (1859–1935), who was of Jewish descent, for treason in December 1894, which led to a political scandal that dominated French political life until 1906.

171 Abd el-Krim (1882–1963), leader of a revolt against the Spanish Protectorate in Morocco, which result in the Republic of the Rif between 1921 and 1926. France intervened on the Spanish side.

172 Édouard Daladier (1884–1970), Prime Minister of France 1938-1940 (and on earlier occasions). Daladier's position during the war, including time spent in Buchenwald, allowed him to return to the Chamber of Deputies between 1946 and 1958. Maurice Gamelin (1872–1958), Commander-in-chief of the French Armed Forces at the outbreak of WWII.

the F.F.I.[173]—soon gave up trying to imitate *"les soldats de l'an II"*[174]; the regular army was so strapped for volunteers that the "pacification" of Viet Nam and Morocco has had to be mostly conducted by a Foreign Legion recruited from German war prisoners, Russian deserters, Poles and Italians. The Communists know very well how unpopular and antiquated militarism has become in France. And so, although they are in principle the advocates of a strong "people's army," a big air force and the annexation of the left bank of the Rhine, they do not press these demands very hard. (Or perhaps, who knows, they are waiting until they occupy the War Ministry to uncover their batteries?) In any case, it seems improbable that militarism can be revived in France as a popular institution.

2. France As a Great Power

French economy has been stagnant a long time. And yet, although it began to slow down as early as the revocation of the Edict of Nantes[175] (which facilitated the British economic hegemony that was formalized at Utrecht in 1713), French commerce and industry managed to retain its place in the front ranks up to the end of the Second Empire. Nor should it be forgotten that, despite all the setbacks in its "economic progress," France was always a prosperous country, especially in the sense that a certain ease in living arrangements—dare I say, a certain *"douceur de vivre"*?—was more real and more widespread than in the Germany of Krupp and perhaps even than in the USA—not to mention Japan—despite the more powerful structure of those nations' economies. Even in the sinister 1938–9 period of the liquidation of the Popular Front by Daladier and the Cagoulards[176], might one not have said, in the words of the Swiss banker, Clavieu, who wrote his Amsterdam clients on the eve of the great

---

173 Forces Françaises de l'Interieur: formal name for the French Resistance in the latter period of the Second World War.

174 Translates to "the soldiers of Year II", a reference to the revolutionary armies during the French Revolution.

175 In 1598, King Henry IV of France granted civil rights and religious freedom to Protestants. However, in 1685, King Louis XIV of France revoked the Edict and outlawed Protestantism.

176 La Cagoule: a French fascist terrorist group active from 1936, and headed by Eugène Deloncle (1890–1944).

1789 bankruptcy: "The finances of this country present a mixture of debts and payments, an abundance of cash, a general activity, a goodness of soil, and a geographical situation, all of which combine to make up an incalculable force of resistance." Today, however, if recent economic articles in *Combat* [177] are to be trusted, this fortunate combination of forces of resistance is exhausted, and a period of misery and decay is to be expected: inadequate forces to repair the ruins of war; financial and administrative disorder; decline in real wages; rise in parasitic classes; shortage of labour in industry and agriculture which only heavy immigration of foreign workers can remedy.

As for the roots of France's present political weakness, they may be traced back to 1918 when she was offered a lucky chance, by the collapse of the empires of the Habsburgs, Hohenzollerns and Romanovs, to regain her rank as the leading continental power. It is hardly necessary to rehash here the dismal story of how successive French governments—of the "Right" and "Left" alike—backed by public opinion, threw away this miraculous opportunity. It is strange to recall today how willing, even ardent, the Czechs, the Poles, the Rumanians and the Yugoslavs were to submit to French guidance, how easy it was to come to an understanding with pre-fascist Italy, how Germany itself would have been glad to see its weak democracy supported and advised by a generous republican neighbor, how much more readily the Soviet Union—in the time of Chicherin and Rakovsky[178]—would have reached an understanding with Paris than with London. It was all ruined by ten years of confusion, of pettiness, of indifference by the French "public" to European questions, of squalid adventures (project to restore the Hapsburgs, support given to fascism) and of usurious calculations (reparations). By 1936—after she had rejected the last chance offered her by the Ethiopian war and the Spanish civil war—France had been reduced to a bloated body, spineless, frightened, drifting in the tow of Chamberlain and Halifax, despised—and soon detested—by countries which fifteen years earlier would have been glad to be her satellites.

---

177 A newspaper of the French Resistance that ran from 1941 to 1974.
178 Georgy Chicherin (1872–1936), Soviet politician, active especially in Foreign Affairs, who died (naturally) in 1936. Christian Rakovsky (1873–1941), Soviet politician and diplomat, who fell from favour due to his association with Trotsky and was executed.

What is really discouraging is that in the year 1947 the popularly elected leaders who govern France and the journalistic choir which hymns their deeds for the benefit of the man in the street appear to have learned nothing and forgotten nothing about the ambitions and methods of Poincaré, Tardieu and Georges Bonnet.[179] General DeGaulle is ambitious to play the role of both Foch and Clemenceau[180], a role which was outmoded even in their day. The Ph.D. in history, M. Bidault[181], who goes to mass and is of good family, does indeed lack the vulgarity of the of the Ph.D. in history, M. Daladier, but his political "style" is the same: delay, suspicion, shopkeeper's haggling. And if the pastrycook, Duclos, or the "man of the people," Thorez, were to get power, one could hope for no improvement, not because—as the chauvinists of *Le Populaire*[182] reiterate—they are "agents of a foreign power," but because Stalin's imperialistic policies are disastrous for all peoples, including the Russians.

From now on, Warsaw, Prague, and Belgrade are closed even to the "goodwill tours" of the uninspired Ivon (*sic*) Delbos[183]. Poor Nenni's[184]

---

179 Raymond Poincaré (1860–1934) and André Tardieu (1876–1945), pre-war conservative politicians. Georges Bonnet (1889–1973), a pre-war Radical who supported the Vichy regime. Readmitted to the Radical Party in 1952, he was allowed to run for office again and only lost his seat in the Chamber of Deputies in 1968.

180 Ferdinand Foch (1851–1929), French general who led the final offensive that led to Germany's surrender in WWI. Georges Clemenceau (1841–1929), Prime Minister of France during the final years of WWI.

181 Georges Bidault (1899–1983), MRP (see p. 75) politician who headed an alliance government of the MRP, the Socialists and the Communists in late 1946, later returning as Prime Minister 1949–1950. He held other high offices. Later an opponent of Algerian independence.

182 Jacques Duclos and Maurice Thorez were Communist politicians. Caffi is slightly wrong in calling Thorez "man of the people" — his 1938 biography was *Fils du people*, "Son of the People". *Le Populaire* was the daily paper of the French Socialist party, the SFIO and very briefly the PS: published 1918–1970.

183 Yvon Delbos (1885–1956), Radical Party politician who visited Warsaw, Bucharest, Belgrade and Prague in December 1937 seeking to foster political friendship with France, in his role as the Popular Front government's Minister of Foreign Affairs.

184 Pietro Nenni (1891–1980), veteran Italian Socialist leader. Between the end of the Second World War and the Hungarian Revolution of 1956 he favoured strong ties between Italy's Socialists and Communists, a policy which caused a scission in the Italian Socialist Party.

outstretched hand of friendship seems likely to remain in mid-air, while in Italy the brief period of Francophilia has already soured to resentment. Neither the Anglo-Americans nor the Russians, confident in their own power, use any ceremony when they want to manipulate France (or one part of France strong enough to neutralize the other). And yet the very idea of a European problem, of international solidarity based on something more solid than rhetoric appears to be totally absent from the mental horizon of the men who govern France. A few journalissts (*sic*) now and then speak in such terms, knowing very well they are voices in the wilderness. And His Majesty, the Proletariat? Majestically, he says the hell with it.

3. The Sun of French Culture

Culturally, France has maintained a position of leadership more or less continuously from Descartes to Proust, Gide and Halévy[185], and now to the Paris School in painting and such writers as Malraux.[186] Ignorant though I am of London and New York as centers of culture, I venture to state that Paris has not been dethroned, that intellectuals like Camus and Sartre[187] can measure up to any rivals on the international scene, and that France still has an incomparable elite of talented writers and a flourishing "literary life" of taste, vitality, and large human spirit.

This cultural position is based on (1) certain general features of world civilization, and (2) certain French cultural and social institutions. That both—or either—will survive can no longer be taken for granted.

(1) Doubtless the absolute number of persons in the world today who speak French is greater than it has ever been. But relative to other tongues, the world-domain of French has shrunk. In Diderot's[188] time, French culture was practically coterminous with Western culture, and its

---

185 Élie Halevy (1870–1937), French philosopher and historian.

186 André Malraux (1901–1976), novelist, Gaullist politician, Resistant, and fighter for the Republic in the Spanish civil war. Minister for Cultural Affairs from 1958 to 1969.

187 Albert Camus (1913–1960) and Jean-Paul Sartre (1905–1980), both were French philosophers, novelists, activists, and critics.

188 Denis Diderot (1713–1784), writer and philosopher. Key figure in the "Enlightenment".

votaries throughout Europe were very nearly the total group of "cultivated persons." Today languages more widely spoken than French have become the instruments of a popular education that is thought to be on as high a level—and more "up-to-date"—than that formerly drawn from French writings. No French book can possibly achieve the huge printings common in Russia and America, the two nations which have chiefly developed that kind of mass or popular culture which spreads farther throughout the world every day. France herself is already half swamped: Hollywood films are shown widely, and it appears that translations of American and British novels are read in greater numbers than the works of French authors. It is not likely that French intellectuals and artists can harmonize their work with this sort of "popular culture"—or rather, substitute for culture—nor that the products of French culture, saturated as they are with individualism and humanism, can successfully compete with it.

So far, I have spoken only of literature. But literature is far from constituting the total of those cultural values whose diffusion has illuminated the name of France. Intellectual tendencies are closely connected with trends in all sorts of other fields, from the sublime to the frivolous. The diffusion of French thought is accompanied by the diffusion of all kinds of useful and pleasurable objects, of hairdressing styles and jewels, of military titles, of rules of etiquette, of recipes and table manners. In the age of tanks, cocktails, pullover sweaters, bars, week-ends, etc., the lead in social customs and the whole *décor* of living has more and more come from outside France. Perhaps Russian fashions will now have their turn, and *Humanité* [189] will soon be telling us that the samovar is the genial invention of Stalin's grandfather, who was punished by the cruel Czarist government for daring, like a modern Prometheus, to bring the people hot water for collective consumption.

(2) The peculiar qualities of French high culture, both works of art and intellectual productions, are closely linked to two features of French social organization: the educational system, and a tradition of sociability.

France has long had a remarkable system of schools and colleges: the Sorbonne, the Academy, the Jesuit colleges, the strict and thorough

---

189 *L'Humanité,* newspaper: Founded by Jean Jaurès in 1904 as a Socialist paper, it became the organ of the French Communist Party. It is still published.

secondary schools, and the great Napoleonic foundations: *Ecole Polytechnique, Ecole Normale*, and the various *Ecoles des Beaux Arts*[190], which, reactionary as they have often been, have always taught the highest standards of craftsmanship. For over a century this system, whose chief emphasis has been laid on serious study and on developing the ability to express one's own ideas with ease and clarity, has been the nursery of an intellectual elite which it has at the same time thoroughly tested and sifted (*"le jeune francais—bête à concours"*).[191] The Third Republic added a compulsory primary-school system to which, outside the official bureaucratic plans and often in direct opposition to them, the republican enthusiasm of a whole class of humble intellectuals imbued with the idea of being the avant garde of the advancing people was able to give a spirit of large humanitarianism and liberating anticlericalism which contrasted sharply with the work of the famous "Prussian schoolmaster, architect of Sadowa, Sedan..."[192] and Hitler.

The other great tap-root of French culture is a *sociability* that is probably unequalled since the symposia, the agoras and the porticos of the Greek city states. This has made conversation a necessity of everyday life—a conversation that observes a code of politeness whose first article is the complete equality of the talkers, and that pursues only one end: clear expression and understanding. A novel by Louis Bertrand[193] notes that in a small city of eastern France in 1870 there might still be observed all the social usages of the thousands of salons that had grown up in imitation of the court at Versailles. The proliferation is uninterrupted from the salon of the Marquise de Rambuillet to those "cafes litteraires" which André Billy[194] has recently written about with such nostalgia.

---

190 All examples of the 'Grandes Écoles', where the French elite is trained and networks. This is also true of the *École des Sciences Politiques* mentioned below.

191 [Caffi's footnote]: "French youth—examination fodder."

192 This is a reference to Helmuth von Moltke the Elder (1800–1891), Prussian field marshal who designed a more modern method for directing armies.

193 Louis Bertrand (1866–1941), French novelist. The novel most likely being mentioned by Caffi is *L'Invasion* (1907), which depicts the experiences of French people during the Franco-Prussian War.

194 Catherine de Vivonne, marquise de Rambouillet (1588–1665), host of an important 17th century literary *salon* that is sometimes considered to be the

How much is left today of the backbone of the Napoleonic *Université* and of these real organs of French sociability? The papers are full of complaints about the educational crisis: professors and teachers are driven by hunger to look for a less miserable existence in journalism, administrative posts, or even business. The Vichy regime upset the normal-school system, where teachers are prepared, and as a result it may be that the whole spirit of primary instruction has been altered. Furthermore, the ascendance of the Communist Party has substituted dogmatic conformism and the cult of the State in those teaching circles whose attitude used to be libertarian; while the clerical reactionaries who were favored by Vichy have used the power of the MRP[195] to hold the positions they won at that time. Whether it is a question of the intellectual level of candidates for a B.A., or of the living conditions of college fellows, or of the superficial and botched-up reorganization of the *Ecole des Sciences Politiques* (the traditional fortress of reaction), or of the abandoning of the study of Greek (and Latin, too, before long, it seems likely), or of hospital internes and laboratory assistants who are now faced with actual hunger unless they have independent incomes—wherever one looks, the sad state of French education is evident. It has become almost impossible for the younger generation to acquire the kind of intellectual training which their elders received at the beginning of their careers. Another factor is the corruption that hangs heavy in the contemporary atmosphere and that attracts youth to the black market or other forms of easy-money parasitism. Above all, there is the widespread tendency to prefer technological training to the "folderol" of the humanities. This reduction of knowledge to a utilitarian instrument is one more instance of the triumph of mass culture.

As for sociability, I can make no final judgment, since we still live "in temporary quarters," after the earthquake which uprooted so many lives and conditioned so many people to look with bitter suspicion on their neighbors and to lose all scruples about getting the better of them. One

---

birthplace of French salon culture. André Billy (1882–1971), French novelist and literary critic.

195 MRP—Mouvement Républicaine Populaire: French Christian Democratic party important in the decade after the Second World War. Although initially drawn from resistants, its tendency to be a vehicle for right wing politicians with ties to the Vichy, noted here by Caffi, became a feature of the party. It gradually dwindled and entered a process of mergers.

can imagine the pleasures and the tastes of the only class that today is prosperous: those enriched by speculation, collaboration and black market deals, which persist despite the thunderbolts of M. Ives Farge's[196] cartoons.

Civilizations do indeed die, as Paul Valéry[197] writes; but he might have added that they take their time about it. After all, students were writing impeccable Attic Greek under the last Byzantine emperors; and if it is hard to remember that the Anglo-Danish buffoon[198] who now rules Greece is the legitimate successor of Theseus (a Theseus who has brought back with him the Minotaur and given it his people for a pasture), when we hear Venizelos or Politis[199] debate, we sense the heritage of Odysseus, the man of many counsels. And so it would be premature to assume that Paris and French culture are in permanent decline—although I must say that Malraux's prophecies, in his pathetic UNESCO address, seemed excessively subjective.

4. French Empire to "Union Francaise"

During his term as premier, Leon Blum made many speeches. The reader of the thick volume containing them will find not a sentence, not an allusion to the 50 or 60 million colonial subjects of the Third Republic, nothing on the bloody repressions in North Africa in 1937-8, nothing on the Indochinese atrocities and the scandalous famine of 1931-2, nothing on the wretchedness and slavery André Gide found in French Equatorial Africa. For it was Blum who once said: "I am a Frenchman first, a socialist afterwards." And it was the *Front National* government which sent the "tough" General Nogues[200] to Morocco, which refused amnesty to the

---

196 Yves Farge (1899-1953), an independent leftist politician involved in the Resistance, a government minister in 1946, and very active in opposing wine smuggling and the like. Close to the PCF.

197 Paul Valéry (1871-1945), French essayist and philosopher.

198 Whether this was King George or King Paul of Greece depends on when in 1947 Caffi wrote this, as Paul succeeded George in April that year. As they were brothers both fit the criteria of "Anglo-Danish buffoon".

199 Sofoklis Venizelos (1894-1964) and Athanese George Politis (1893-1968), Greek political figures of this era.

200 General Charles Noguès (1876-1971), sentenced for treason during the Second World War in 1947 *in absentia.*

Indochinese political prisoners confined in the hell of Poulo Condor[201], and which approved the mass executions in Morocco and Tunisia.

All this suggests the abyss between democratic France and that overseas Empire which is now supposed to feel united to the "mother country" by common memories and shared glories. In reality, throughout most of the Third Republic, colonial expansion had three purposes: (1) to keep far away from Paris those militarists who were, by reason of their politics or their ambition, most dangerous to the existence of the republic (such as the monarchist, Lyautey[202]); (2) to make profits for a plutocracy which got its start under Gambetta[203] and which went in for the kind of shady deals Tardieu's African companies and the Bank of Indochina practiced on a large scale; (3) to soothe those nationalistic feelings of the middle and petty bourgeoisie which had been ulcerated by the 1870 defeat. The nation as a whole began to profit from the colonies only with World War I, when several hundred thousand African natives were slaughtered on the Western Front as a sacrifice to the tribal gods of Law and Civilization. After 1919, the colonial contribution to French prosperity became considerable: the Indochinese rubber boom, the huge profits from Moroccan plantations, the West African cocoa industry—all these made their contribution to the French budget and even, as in England in the 19th century, made possible a modest rise in workingclass living standards.

But we should not forget that, alongside the France which has developed the bourgeois spirit to its farthest imaginable reaches of egotism, greed, spite, treachery, and antisocial meanness, there exists also another France—one of uncompromising intelligence, of a sociability filled with uncalculating *gentilesse* and a kind of romantic boldness, eager for adventures not in a "superman" spirit, but rather in the temper shown by Joinville's[204] companions when they said during the battle in the desert "that this will be something interesting to tell our ladies about"; the France which cannot bear to have a single person suffer injustice, be it the

---

201 Now known as the Côn Đáo Islands, off the south coast of Vietnam.
202 Hubert Lyautey (1854–1934), French general and colonial administrator, notably Resident-General of France in Morocco, 1907–1925, and also Minister of War, Dec 1916–Mar 1917.
203 Léon Gambetta (1838–1882), Republican politician in the late 19th century Third Republic, Prime Minister of France 1881–1882.
204 Probably François d'Orléans, prince de Joinville, (1818–1900).

protestant Calas[205] or the Jew Dreyfus, the France which—in the past, anyway—went to the barricades at the cry "Vive la Pologne!" (This dualism—sometimes observable in the same individual—is the real tragedy of French "social mythology.") It was only the French who fraternized with the North American redskins, and it was in France that the cry rang out, apropos the abolition of slavery: "*Périssent les colonies, plûtot qu'un principe!*"[206] Thus, in the simplest way, without either Quaker doctrines or philanthropic texts, French intellectuals (and no doubt many others who are not known to us) looked on natives as human beings and needed no *raison d'Etat* to protest against their oppression and urge them to defend themselves.

It is true that it, in our times, the intellectuals and the sincere democrats of France have made no headway, or very little, in getting the government to treat the colonial peoples with justice and generosity.[207] And yet the "idées claires" in which the French idiom is so rich—especially the political idiom—have frequently set in into motion quite unexpected forces. The very formula, "Union Francaise," written into official texts has already provoked a fermentation which can be bottled up neither by the disavowals of politicians nor the brutalities of that Carmelite admiral recently sent to Indochina to defend the opium and alcohol monopoly. They can massacre the Annamites, they can play on the fear or corruption of the notables of Cochin-China[208], but they cannot wipe away the fact that they [were] treated as equals with the government of Viet-Nam (which

---

205 The Calas affair, centring on the trial, torture and execution of the protestant Jean Calas in Toulouse, happened between 1761 and 1765.

206 Translates to "Let the colonies perish, rather than a principle!"

207 [Caffi's footnote]: This inability of "thinking France," despite its great influence on public opinion, to insinuate its ideas into the actual functioning of the State machinery is a point worth reflecting about. It was strikingly manifested in the Constituent Assembly of 1789–91, all of whose good intentions were so easily nullified in action—as, for instance, the paper system of local self-government which the Jacobins suppressed in practice. Another example was the 1944 "liberation": new men, animated by generous visions, apparently came to the top—and yet the machinery of the State, more weighty and fantastic than ever, is once more lumbering along, brushing aside like straws the most solemn promises of a New Order. And it is the Men of the Resistance themselves, the very ones who then appeared so ardent for change, who today drive, pull, or push the sinister mechanism along.

208 An archaic colonial term for the Southern part of Vietnam.

seems to be headed by a most remarkable man[209]). The Algerian government appears to have successfully falsified the elections in many districts, but the voice of the Arab and Berber separatists has already been heard and will be heard in the Palais Bourbon.[210] Grotesque as may be the concession of a single deputy for a district of one million square miles, and however "backward" may be the natives of West and Equatorial Africa, they realize that something new is in the air, that forced labor is officially abolished and that one can even, with circumspection, oppose the Whites who only yesterday were still so all-mighty. All this will no doubt develop in confusion and fantastic suffering, but it does seem that a real social and political emancipation is now in progress. In any event, the French colonial empire has lived out its sordid life.

5. 1789 and 1947

I cannot forget the sorrowful words of that Spanish Republican colonel who saw his comrades shut up by Daladier in the Gurs prison camp[211]: "The France that we loved and respected has been dead since 1870."

Let us attempt to distinguish between the misconceptions and the true insights comprised in that experience of disillusionment that occurs so often—and not only in our time—when some friend of the France of the Encyclopedists and of the Revolution comes up against quite another France, one of the most pettifogging "ésprit bourgeois," of insufferable chauvinist vanity, of bureaucratic cretinism and the desiccated inhumanity of an obtuse "common sense." What connection, indeed, can be established between such national traits and the generous principles of 1789-92?

To begin with, it is interesting to note that these principles, although formulated in a more rigorously logical system than that of British liberalism or American democracy, have yet, in their diffusion throughout the world, had a much stronger emotional appeal. When the native elites of "backward" nations admire the British constitution, when some Latin

---

209 Presumably Ho Chi Minh.
210 i.e. the French National Assembly.
211 After the Spanish Civil War, many soldiers fled to France, only to be interned, particularly at Gurs in southern France, in harsh conditions.

American or Philippine government proposes to imitate the American system, it is a matter of doctrinaire pronouncements and of mimicry of external rules of political conduct. But for those who in the 19th century considered France their "second fatherland"—and for contemporary revolutionaries in Madagascar and Vietnam—adherence to the principles of Liberty, Equality, Fraternity as understood in 1789, 1830, 1848, and 1870 is transmuted into an enthusiasm which embraces a whole *Weltanschauung;* a revolution in each individual's most intimate being and in his own personal fate.

I believe I am correct in saying that the majority of Americans accept more wholeheartedly and completely the principles of their 1776–1785 revolution than is the case with the majority of Frenchmen with *their* revolutionary principles of 1789. For to accept (and, indeed, to insist on) the principles of the American Revolution means to reach the heights of respectable conformity, ultimately arriving at the stratospheric respectability of the Daughters of the American Revolution.[212] While until very recently in France, and still more so in countries dominated by France, any appeal to the principles of 1789 inevitably took on the rebellious color of a call to battle against the status quo in order to "complete the work begun by the Revolution." When the appeal was serious, that is. When it was exploited in official speeches, the popular suspicion was that it was all a demagogic trick. The principles of 1776 have been satisfactorily (to 99 out of 100 Americans, at least) embodied in stable institutions which may be criticised or amended only in minor details. But the principles embodied in the French constitution of 1791, although in content much the same as those set forth in the American Declaration of Independence, have always been interpreted by those who passionately believed in them as the very promise of Utopia; and the institutions which were supposed to embody them have been ephemeral not only because the forces of reaction have been persistent and strong in France, but even more because in the eyes of their partisans those principles have been merely preliminary sketches whose true realization lay in the future. To sum up: the principles of the American Revolution crystallized a society simple in structure and homogeneous in its moral and social code; but the Rights of Man subverted a feudal, Catholic,

---

212 Organisation for women descended from participants—on the 'rebel' side—
  in the American War of Independence.

hierarchical and repressive social order while at the same time it called into existence a kind of popular and equalitarian "sociability" with which I can find nothing to compare in the modern world.[213] It is, therefore, not surprising that the "tradition of 1789" should be a complicated and contradictory affair.

EUROPEAN

(Translated by Dwight Macdonald)

---

213 [Caffi's Footnote]: To say nothing of the complexity of the purely ideological elements which went into the making of "the principles of 1789," as contrasted with the relative harmony of the various Anglo-Saxon ideologies. It was apparently not too difficult to find a workable compromise between the rationalism of Locke and the individualistic (and often libertarian) ideas of the Puritans, the Wesleyans and the other non-conformist sects. But consider, on the other hand, such antinomies as Rabelais-Calvin, Montaigne-Saint François de Sales, Descartes-Pascal, Voltaire-Rousseau—antinomies which have carried to the point of paroxysm the consciousness of an irreducible (*sic*) disharmony in the "French point of view" about the basic problems of human destiny and social justice.

On Mythology [214]

By "myths" everybody seems to mean those creations of the collective mind which take the form of tales, dances, ritual representations and symbols of all sorts in societies designated as "primitive." In these societies are found in undifferentiated state all those elements which "later on" appear in autonomous form as religious experience, metaphysical speculation, pure artistic creation, magical and then rational science, and perhaps even as systems of morality, law, politics, and ecclesiastical organization.

According to Roger Caillois [215] (Frazer and Lévy-Bruhl [216] would perhaps have been of the same opinion), the myth dies, that is to say, loses its "reality" (its efficacy as magic, ritual, norm) in "literature." For Caillois, Plato's myths were already "literature" since Plato did not "believe" them.

It seems to me that far from dying, the myth becomes more complex when the different forms of art, religious dogma, philosophy and science offer it diversified masks, so often bewildering by their cunning elaboration or audacious spontaneity. Moreover, the myth is peculiarly at work when the pressures of rigorous rationalism, of strictly revealed or demonstrated "truth," of political, moral and aesthetic conformism come into conflict with the need to communicate with one's fellows.

As to the fact of "belief" (in supernatural powers, gods, demons, etc.), there is scarcely a break between the primitive myths and, let us say, those of Plato, or the tales Herodotus introduces with the remark: "You may believe as much of this as you like." (Had he not told these stories we

---

214 Article published in *possibilities*, 1, Winter 1947/8. Billed as "An Occasional Review" this journal only published one edition.

215 Roger Caillois, (1913–1978), French writer. A key figure in the *Collège de Sociologie* with Georges Bataille, a Parisian group which gave public lectures between 1937 and 1939. Caffi may have been involved to some extent with this group. See Marco Bresciani, *La rivoluzione perduta*, pp. 211–212.

216 Sir James George Frazer, (1854–1933). Scottish anthropologist, and notably author of *The Golden Bough*. Lucien Lévy-Bruhl, (1854–1933), French anthropologist.

should not know half as much as we do about the "reality," that is, the mentality, the interests, the infrastructures, etc. of the Hellenic or barbarian societies he sketched for us in living images.)

From the very beginning the myth has been a representation and, above all, a communication of "things that do not exist but *are*." For by the sole fact that it is put in the form of a story or symbol, the myth excludes from actual existence the beings, the events, the norms of conduct, the fortunes and misfortunes that constitute its content: these either were present in the world when "I wasn't there" or are present in a world different from the one in which "I exist." The realm of the myth has rightly been called "sacred." Now the sacred is beyond attachment, incomprehensible (recalling the original sense of the word *comprehendere*: to seize), ineffable. And the whole effect of the myth — inseparable from active magic or passive mysticism — is to touch, to make present (by fiat or insinuation), to symbolize (the symbol was a sign of recognition or alliance) the ineffable by means of the word, "the nonexistent," by means of the assertion: "Once Upon a time there *was*...," or "In a far-off land, separated from us by seven seas and thirty countries, there *is*. . ." The paradox is that without this "nonexistent" our existence would have no human significance, as without the ineffable, human speech would scarcely differ from the vocal expression of animals.

Some mark off a "mythological age," arguing that the obsession with the "sacred" and the spirit of participation are found only among primitives, that "civilized" people repress the "dream-level" and think and act in entire accordance with the "critical" views of experience and logic. Is this true? I do not think any of us is capable of eliminating every emotional coefficient — the "coefficient of adversity," for instance — and hence all spirit of participation from his relations with people and with things.... Each of us can no doubt recall some occasion when he had to exert his whole capacity for action, self-control and determination, in order to achieve a given end; the thing done, did one not have the feeling that success came by a miracle, that it would be impossible to say with certainty why this shift worked and that did not, or how it came about that this possibility was suddenly suggested, that circumstance as mysteriously overlooked? No doubt the primitive hunter had reactions of this sort every time he killed an animal. What is more to the point, in the memoirs of soldiers of Napoleon we find allusions to such experience for every cavalry charge. (Tolstoi, in *War and Peace*[217], describes with great precision how Nicholas Rostov became aware that the "right" moment had come to throw in his squadron.) And is there an avowal of lover or artist (Benvenuto Cellini[218] casting his Perseus) which does not lie out of sincere emotion?

To me it seems evident that the paradoxes of the "true-and-false" and the "nonexistent" that "is," traverse the whole of our life, pertain to the human condition as such and cannot be historically segregated.

Of course there are differences, due to the changing situations in the social network. For one thing, in a primitive milieu, states of torpor (as with animals) bring utter passivity, forgetfulness of existence. While the routine of the hunter, like that of the farmer and artisan, involves the continual presence of factors of "good and ill luck," the observation of signs in one's surroundings and in things, presentiments and precautions of a magical order. Finally, work done in harness, the passive obedience of the soldier, the "activity" of the bureaucrat, the feverish compulsions of the business man to whom "time is money," all admit of a mental torpor *in the very heart of productive existence....* (Here is perhaps the meaning of the famous curse: "You shall live by the sweat of your brow": that is, in the enforced forgetfulness of nonexistential realities.)

Then, solitude and disorientation among men and happenings "completely strange to me" are rare exceptions among primitives; they are all almost the rule in "civilized" agglomerations. So that the mythological experience has to turn inward, to put on an armor of diffidence and individuality (closely bordering on mental alienation), and while remaining very virulent in the depths of consciousness, is able to communicate itself only rarely and with difficulty, and then more by means of the "interior dialogue" than by the direct sense of the spoken word.

---

217 *War and Peace*, (1869), is one of Tolstoi's major works, and Count Nikolai Rostov is a character in the novel, who gives up his studies to become a Hussar in the Russian war against Napoleon's invading forces.

218 Benvenuto Cellini (1500–1571), Italian sculptor whose famous bronze statue *Perseus with the Head of Medusa* was made between 1545 and 1554. It is currently housed in the Loggia dei Lanzi in Florence.

Another difference between integral mythology and differentiated (or "dispersed") mythology should be noted. Roger Fry[219] said of the painters of the paleolithic caves that their amazing capacity to "see" the mammoth or the bison in a living mass, outside of all arrangements of perspective, of proportions and details, was lost when man became a "geometer," able to measure and dissociate what he perceives (this would date from the neolithic period). I have also read somewhere that children have a vision of things which consists of embracing them completely with a single glance, but when they learn to read, to beak (*sic*)[220] down words into letters, they lose this faculty. This makes one recall how Plato deplored the invention of writing; he had in mind not the visual effects of letters but the dissociation of language from the sacred (only partial, I should say) implied by writing, a process similar to what happens to drawing when, from having been instinctive, it becomes "deliberate." Undoubtedly, the language of the "unlettered" is a perpetual process of creation, while written language congeals both the form and meaning of each word; and the oral tradition, afire with immediate inspiration and improvisation, has a vitality unmatched by the tradition of the "book."...

Lévy-Bruhl, in line with other ethnologists whom he cites, has insisted on the importance to Australian tribes of the places connected with the periodic rites, the genealogical and cosmogenic legends, the prohibitions and the ordinances of each clan; each man feels himself to be in a state of "participation" with the hills and even with the cardinal points in his native "place," as with the animals and plants which he assimilates to his kin or ancestors; this is why the expulsion of a tribe from its "place," a thing which appears of such little consequence to the British administration, results in a real disintegration of the community so treated. The tribesmen abandon their rites and norms of behavior, yielding to a kind of collective despair. Spanish doctors have studied a similar illness which seems to afflict the Galicians inhabiting the coast bordering on Portugal; the Galician emigré is stricken with a nostalgia of such violent character that he languishes and often dies; no physiological

219 Roger Fry (1866-1934), English painter and art critic.
220 A typographical error, presumably meaning 'break'.

cause for this ailment has been discovered, and it is all the more surprising in view of the fact that the Galicians are an extremely enterprising and businesslike race.

I wonder if all this (and what the sea may mean to the sailor, the steppe to the Cossack) can be considered as simple epiphenomena of inveterate habits, or be explained as the sentimental tendency of the primitive or "naive" mind to be dominated by the locale instead of mastering it for productive ends.

The Melanesian who has constructed a canoe with consummate care for all the details, the choice of the tree, the drying of the wood, the modeling and planing of the inside and outside, the exact measurement of all the gear, will never believe that his mastery of the matter he has thus transformed has been sufficient to make the boat seaworthy. The "mana" must still prove favorable; for in the tree he felled, in the tools he employed, in the very forms that a long tradition prescribed for the vessel, and even in the resistance of the water, not to speak of winds and storms, there is a multitude of *Dinge an sich*[221] in which he feels that he participates, but which remain none the less disturbing, since they are as capable of hostility as of benevolence. Propitiatory rites are in his judgment as productive as the "labor-time" incorporated in the useful object. When starting on a voyage, he never forgets to conform to customs which economic rationalism would condemn as a waste of time and labor. We should not find this strange. Since the first stone implement the things fashioned by man have solicited his attention (his prudence, his fears, his hopes of "success"), in their metaphysical as in their practical aspects. "At the start you control the machine, but later the machine controls you," a mechanic has noted. The electrician, the aviator, expert in their special skills, find themselves unable to repress a feeling that the complicated mechanisms they handle, and which they know by heart, have, despite everything, a "life" of their own, which it is necessary to placate as well as to control; and they see that the perfidious play of "luck" has a strange reality. The Army, the Administration, the Church are vastly complex machines, and the officer, the bureaucrat, and the priest, are dominated by the conviction (more or less avowed) that

---

221 Lit. "Things in themselves".

these institutions have "existential" value above and beyond the practical ends they serve: they are because they are....

(One must be Benedetto Croce[222] to believe that the work of art is "complete" in the mind of the artist, like the homunculus in the sperm, according to the embryologists of the seventeenth century.[223] The nature of marble, bronze, wood, colors, sounds and words exacts definite forms, limiting the range of the expressible, at times augmenting it with possibilities that miraculously coincide with conscious intent. There is further the action of models: Malraux has justly said that each work of art proceeds from some other work. Evidently what is in play here is something very different from "imitation," which could only yield a progressive impoverishment of the "original" effort. In the work of art which has inspired him, the artist has caught a glimpse of not yet realized possibilities, he has become aware of mythological depths only a fraction of whose rich store has been so far revealed, and which he dares to think a keener glance might yet embrace in its totality...)

Naturally the worker, whose fatigue is accompanied by the most deadly boredom, is scarcely able to cast a magical halo about his task, or see his situation in "mythological" perspective.... Yet the fact is that to obtain the "enthusiastic consent" or even the resignation of the masses to a faster tempo of productive work, it was necessary in Stalin's Russia as in Hitler's Germany, to instil typical *Ersatz* mythologies: vague expectations of an earthly paradise in which everyone would own a car, a radio, an electric stove; sentiments à la Michael Strogoff[224]: "For God!, for Tsar! for Russia!"; perspectives appealing to "sporting blood" or low resentment: "We'll surpass America"; or "We'll get even with the Jews! We'll fix the Poles who stabbed us in the back and robbed us in 1918!" etc., etc.... It is not impossible that in cannibalistic Pan-Germanism[225], in the Sovietism idolizing the social "apparatus" and machines of steel, in Japanese

---

222 Benedetto Croce (1866–1952), Italian philosopher.

223 This discredited theory posited that sperm contained a miniature, preformed organism that would essentially just grow in size within the womb.

224 Apparently a reference to French writer Jules Verne's 1876 novel *Michel Strogoff* (translated as *Michael Strogoff: The Courier of the Czar*).

225 The idea that all Germanic peoples should unify into a single state. Important in the nineteenth century, it prefigured aspects of National Socialist policy.

Imperialism dreaming of revenge on the whites and "Greater East Asia"[226] — and, despite its grotesqueness — in Italian fascism, there were elements of authentic mythology. Degraded, of course; mythological creation is incompatible with the action of regimented masses. For where there is mass action the currents and rhythms of sentiment linking the individual to his fellows, intelligent communion, the complex and delicate play of sympathies requiring the subtle collaboration of the one who speaks and the one who listens — all elements of the mythopoeic "atmosphere" — are replaced by the brutal command, mechanical obedience, the stupidity of the repeated shout. "The Tartars conquered the world and then forgot about it," this remark by a writer of the eighteenth century gives us an insight into the mythological — hence the cultural, artistic, social, philosophical — sterility of the Mongol masses led by Genghis Khan. The barbarian is defined by his poverty of mythological experience; particularly is this true of the learned, planful barbarian, who, to use the phrase Heine[227] directed against the Prussians, makes himself "vicious through science."

The effects of "Taylorism"[228] and other modes of "rationalizing" work, so successful in a certain sense, show clearly enough that even the iron laws of "technico-economic determinism" are unable to secure for "praxis" a complete victory over the psychological caprices which engender gratuitous gestures. For it is very likely that "waste motion" and nonchalant rhythms arising in the course of productive work originate in magical prejudices, ritual habits, and other fantasies. It is still mythology which is all to blame for the topsy-turviness! The "Taylorite-Stakhanovist"[229] is only a step removed from the Kapo[230] or SS of the

---

226 In 1940, during the Second World War, the Japanese Empire tried to establish a pan-Asian union called the Greater Asia Co-Prosperity Sphere, mainly based on territories it had occupied.

227 Heinrich Heine (1797–1856), German poet and writer.

228 Also known as Scientific Management, a system of work organisation developed by American engineer Frederick Winslow Taylor (1856–1915).

229 The Stakhanovite movement was a feature of the USSR under Stalin from 1935 onwards. It was based on workers who exceeded the 'norms' of production required of them.

230 Kapos were prisoners in the Nazi camp system who worked on administrative tasks or supervised forced labour in conjunction with the SS.

"Concentration-Camp World" which flourished in Germany before and during the war, still flourishes in Siberia, and is coming to the fore again in Cyprus and in Palestine. The Kapo, striking down with his club any prisoner who makes the slightest movement while the roll is being called, and the "Taylorite-Stakhanovist," were both prefigured in the legendary counsel given Tarquin[231] when he wanted to know how to become a leader of men: his advisor lopped with his cane those flowers that insolently raised their head above the level of the grass.... In the Prussian army (as in the carrying out of a Five-Year Plan) error was prohibited (and often published by death); it is true that this rigor was somehow balanced by breadth of view in tolerating the "dispersion" of bombs on school children or masterpieces of Palladio[232], when the idea was to destroy some bridge, as well as by the "rough estimates" accepted by court martials and revolutionary tribunals.... The superfluous it would seem, cannot be divorced from the necessary; the gratuitous gesture enters rational action; chance amalgamates itself to the machine.... In order not to be crushed, a man — and a truly human collectivity — should be able to say that "what must come to pass will not, perhaps," and to feel that a last turn of the wheel might change everything.

Justice is not a myth, and most assuredly not an "intellectual construction"; but without a multiple network of mythological creations, from the proverbs and fables to the utterances of the Sophists, the lamentations of Job, the parables of the Gospel, and the visions of Er[233], the norms and antinomies of the just and the unjust could not be ever-present (acting, defied, violated, avenged) in all the transactions of men and in the infrastructure of society.... Mythology determines the relations between individuals in society (including their "productive" relations), but only insofar as these relations are impregnated with spontaneity and what I would call "human health." Fear and need can stimulate mythological creation, but all evidence shows that famine and fear break the interconnections among men, destroying social intuition and

---

They enjoyed privileges in the camps. The word is now a pejorative in the Jewish community.

231 A reference to Lucius Tarquinius Superbus, 'Tarquin the Proud', (534–509 BCE), final king of Rome, overthrown by the uprising that resulted in the Roman Republic. The episode is recounted by Livy and Herodotus.

232 Andrea Palladio (1508–1580), Italian Renaissance architect.

233 A reference to Plato's Myth of Er, a legend that ends *The Republic*.

discernment. The essential fact is the mechanization of human relations, so that any impulse to reflect on one's acts or to take note of one's surroundings is repressed or deadened, society becoming little more than a well-organized herd. Economic forces, of course, continue to act, but absurd and inexpiable sufferings fill existence.... "Dread" may stimulate the creation of certain myths, but it is only *after* the agony of these moments that men can "invent" what has happened to them. "Dread," as a permanent condition of consciousness, implies intellectual experiences, moral commitments, conflicts of "being" with "existence" and "existence" with "being," which disfigure and destroy mythology, manners and customs, and even the possibility of integrating the "I" in the "we."...

Mythology expresses itself in acts — more generally in the behavior of man towards his fellows, towards his natural surroundings (the landscape, animals), insofar as he preserves his liberty of mind and shows his freedom by coherent speech. Diomedes and Glaucon[234] confronting each other with discourse before fighting do not give up their mythological lucidity....

The "idea" of justice represents the effort of man — become aware of his precarious condition — to maintain in his daily speech and conduct a coherence corresponding to the mythological vision and the customs or manners it sanctifies: it represents the defense of society against the reduction of the human being to the status of a "means" or "thing."... Among the primitives (particularly those studied by Lévy-Bruhl), the "just" is identified with the "normal" and the "unjust" with the "abnormal." Within the limits of the accustomed, the tribesmen reveal a careless and complete cordiality, a joyous confidence; but the least suspicion or fear, contact with the unknown, may bring about a complete reversal of feeling, and bestial ferocity, the most perfidious savagery, soon follows: they are then outside all norms, outside the jurisdiction of "manners," "customs," "justice."...

It is hardly stretching the accepted significance of the term to say that "utopias" belong to the realm of the myth. This holds not only for the

---

234 A reference to an event in Homer's *Iliad,* that took place during the Trojan War. These two warriors challenged each other on the battlefield, only to discover that one of their grandfathers once hosted the other's grandfather. The two men then refused to fight each other and exchanged their armor.

literary and philosophical works falling under this heading, but also for the collective emotions raised by prophecies (often confused) to some passionate hope of redemption or a revolt of the oppressed. However, mythology of itself does not imply "programs" or "techniques" of any sort: programs and techniques (churches, dogmas, political maneuvers, war, an apparatus for giving orders and inflicting pain) subject us to harsh necessities which darken the mythological experience. And let us not forget that when the human being is reduced to the role of a means, the result is most often a system of organized repression aiming at *inhuman* ends....

The dispute between Marx, the sincere Stalinists and Sartre, on the one hand, and Plato, Proudhon, Tolstoi, on the other, concerns precisely the individual whom a disintegrating community has deprived of customs and "adequate" myths. The degenerate city, the reign of "money" and the "stock-exchange," the civilization of machines and endless bustle, seem to Plato, Proudhon, Tolstoi, monstrosities from which one must separate oneself at any price, in order to reshape, if need be by ascetic renunciation, a living soul, founded on justice and the active search for truth. While, Marx — whom we perhaps should not class with those who agree with him — is convinced that if the proletarian is so near to salvation it is precisely because he has nothing but his chains to lose, and among these chains Marx singles out for special condemnation all the residues of mythological creation which he designates as "alienations." It is necessary to annihilate at last all these chimeras, these prejudices, which still block the way to total revolt; a man all new, completely naked, guided by reason alone is necessary for the creation of the "good" society, in which a knowledge of reality, of all reality, and of nothing but reality, shall govern human life. This conception does not lack apocalyptic grandeur. But could one indeed restore or create the "good" society with men who would turn their backs on the substantial elements of all social communion: manners, customs and mythological activity?

The effort towards truth in art, in science, in feelings (sincerity), in social relations (justice), gives an ever renewed vigor to mythological creation, or "experience." But dogmatism, any subjection of the *true* to existential ends, kills the myth. Messianism is just as incompatible with myth as is utilitarian rationalism. In Christianity, mythology is almost exclusively heterodox. Paul of Tarsus[235], with his fanatical insistence on the certainty of salvation through the miracle of the Cross, trampled on many mythological buds of the Gospels and of the first Christian community. In the *Divine Comedy*[236], one senses a conflict between the Catholic who believes in the "real" existence of Heaven and Hell, and the poet who is perfectly aware that he has not by "special grace" seen the kingdoms of Christ and Lucifer; harmony is best established in the *Purgatorio*, where the rich flowering of mythological reminiscences and of Italo-Provençal folklore does not run afoul of "dogmatics" well-padded with Plotinian Hellenism. It is possible that Michelangelo[237] (and this would tally with his sad fate as a "victim of society"), despite a lively feeling (very nostalgic) for the ancient — and heroic — myth of Man, allowed himself to be dominated by the thirst for a "total truth" imperiously established by the God of the two Testaments; and it would perhaps be the traces of his "theological" yearnings which El Greco sensed as weakness in "The Last Judgment."[238] The Church has never tolerated much meditation of the "mysteries" (dogmatically circumscribed). The defects of the Calvinists, Quakers and Methodists — and even our "conscientious objectors" — lies in their assurance of possessing a "simple and total truth," and of thereby being beyond the "pagan temptations" of myth.

Aristotle was too intelligent and too Greek to remove the mythological halo from our knowledge of the world (his remark that poetry is superior to history can serve as proof), but his system, by "explaining everything," certainly favored that anti-mythological DDT[239] of which scholasticism in

---

235 Saint Paul, (C. 5 CE–C. 64/54 CE), Christian apostle and author of several books of the New Testament of the Bible.

236 *The Divine Comedy*, an Italian narrative poem by Dante Alighieri, begun circa 1308 and completed around 1321. The *Purgatorio* alluded to by Caffi is a section of this poem.

237 Michaelangelo, (1475–1564), Italian Sculptor and artist.

238 El Greco, (1541–1614), Greek Painter active in Spain, real name Doménikos Theotokópoulos. 'El Greco' means 'The Greek'. "The Last Judgement" refers to Michaelangelo's painting which El Greco criticised.

239 DDT: Dichlorodiphenyltrichloroethane. An insecticide widely used during and after World War 2, but which—after the publication of Rachel Carson's *Silent Spring* in 1962—came under scrutiny and was, for instance, banned for agricultural use in the USA. There has been a worldwide ban on its agricultural use since 2004, although it still has a limited use in anti-malarial action due to its effectiveness in killing mosquitoes.

general and Thomism[240] in particular were composed. Hegel, without any of Aristotle's inhibitions, brought about analogous results: he thought he could encircle past and future mythology with the barbed-wire of his "dialectic," and his epigones have been able to cook up to their hearts' content ragouts of rationalized and undigested myths and of pseudo-mythologized rationalism. Proudhon's *Justice*[241] is very much impregnated with authentic mythology: "The Man of the People," "the Philosophy of the People," etc. Whereas Marx (as we saw before), desiring at all costs effectively to change the world "such as it is," repudiated almost with hatred mythological motifs (though in *The 18th Brumaire*[242] he too dipped into myth). Bergson[243] desired that his "life force" be an *existing* reality; thus he deprecated mythology. I believe that Sorel[244], when speaking of the "myth" of the general strike, etc., let himself be carried along by Marx and Bergson to a total misunderstanding of the contrast between "myth" and "messianic faith."

Why do I insist on designating as "mythology" what everyone else understands as language, literature, art, religion, philosophy, science, etc.?

First, if there is a common denominator to all activities of the mind and to their "differentiated" creations, a term for this would be useful. But there is an entirely different reason. In language, in customs and superstitions, in all the arts and in philosophy, science, etc., there are a great many manifestations (works) that are *this side* of mythology — all that which is instrumental, determined by the "needs of existence" of the individual in society. And there is also, in art, in religion, in the search for "exact truth," in the antinomies of the moral consciousness, moments that

---

240 Thomism, the philosophical and theological school which arose from the work of Thomas Aquinas (1225–1274).

241 i.e. *De la justice dans la revolution et dans l'église* ('Of Justice in the Revolution and in the Church'), a work of Proudhon's published in 1858.

242 i.e. *The Eighteenth Brumaire of Louis Napoleon*, an essay by Marx originally published in German in 1852, with later versions published as *The Eighteenth Brumaire of Louis Bonaparte.*

243 Henri Bergson, (1859–1941), French philosopher.

244 Georges Sorel, (1847–1922), French social thinker, associated, as Caffi notes, with the notion of 'myth'.

are most certainly *that side of* mythology (the Nirvana, the frenzy of the Cross, the "perfection" of such and such a verse of Racine, such and such a passage of Bach[245], cases of saintliness, heroism, etc.)

The proper field of mythology seems to me to coincide with that of the human communion which I call *society par excellence,* in which the human individual *free from all commitment,* and having to respect neither obligations nor sanctions, is able to overcome "anguish" and "dread" in accepting (if only momentarily) as "realities" forms with regard to which it matters little whether or not they correspond to something in "the world in which I exist."...

Andrea Caffi   (*Translated from French by Lionel Abel*)[246]

---

245 Jean Racine (1639–1699), French dramatist. Johann Sebastian Bach (1685–1750), German composer.

246 Another version of this text, differently ordered and rather longer, appears as "Myth and Mythology" in Andrea Caffi, *A Critique of Violence,* Indianapolis, Bobbs-Merrill, 1970, pp. 177–196. This is dated 1946 at its close.

A Glance at Marx's Horizons[247]

*"Man foresees his destiny through sympathy, and when,
by means of science, he has verified the forecast of
his sympathies, when he has become assured of the
legitimacy of his desires, he advances calmly and
confidently towards the future which is then known
to him. This is how he becomes the free and intelligent
agent of his fate, which he cannot alter (indeed, he
has no such desire) but which he can hasten by his labors".*
(Doctrine of Saint Simon. Exposition. First Year,
1829–2nd Edition, 1830, Vol. 1, p. 121)[248]

Marx and Engels belong to the "scientific mentality" of 1850, which on the one hand reacted *against* Hegelianism, and on the other, resolved to set this philosophy right side up, utilizing its structure but bringing it "down to earth from the celestial regions.[249] Taine[250] and Kenan[251] (*sic*) also snared this effort (in *l'Avenir de la Science* and in *l'Intelligence*): the most rigorous (and for Kenan[252], often the most prudent) methods of philosophy and of physiology (preferably experimental) were to assure the solidity of the foundation. But there was no one who did not recoil before the perspective of a sheer mass of facts (this would be the scientific conception of 1880), and in principle, at least, the achieved totality of the knowable universe was never lost from sight.

---

247 Published in an undated, unpaginated edition of *Instead*, which is generally taken to be edition 1, in early 1948. This edition of the journal does not even have anything in it to identify it as an edition of the journal.

248 This citation can be found in the English translation of *The Doctrine of Saint-Simon: An Exposition. First Year 1828*–1829, translated by G. G. Iggers, Boston, Beacon Press, 1958, p. 39. There should be an ellipsis between the two sentences in the quote above since there are three sentences between them.

249 Presumably a quotation mark has been omitted here.

250 Hippolyte Taine (1828–1893), French philosopher and historian. Published *De l'Intelligence* in 1870.

251 A typographical error for Ernest Renan (1823-1892), French writer, scholar, philosopher and historian. Published *L'Avenir de la science, pensées de 1848* in 1890, though it was written, as implied by the sub-title, in 1848.

252 See last note.

Marx had been stimulated by Feuerbach's[253] "anthropology," with what it implied of a return to the rationalism of the eighteenth century. But what was lacking from the *Deutsche Ideologie*[254], as from the works of Feuerbach, and could scarcely be supplied by an analysis, however penetrating, of general concepts like "human nature," "society," "alienation," "consciousness," was an inventory of precise facts; chemists, biologists, doctors had a long way to go yet before arriving at clear notions like those of a Claude Bernard (and the "views of the whole" of the frankly materialist epigones of Feuerbach: Vogt, Moleschott, Buchner[255], etc. were hasty and platitudinous). We must not neglect to note that the much more critical intellect of Marx could hardly have been satisfied by the ingenious combinations that seemed serviceable to Engels... In any case, serious research in ethnograhpy (*sic*), of such importance for any scientific judgement of the origins of social organization, only began around 1865 (with Taylor[256]). In all this part of the study of social life, "scientific" construction in 1850 was a vague enough notion, and there was little to pit against the Hegelian generalizations (or the generalizations of Saint Simon and Auguste Comte[257]): only a few, poorly verified, empirical fragments... If today these "fragments" have accumulated into masses that seem imposing, let us bear in mind that the masses are still made up of fragments, and it is very doubtful if science will ever close the gaps in our knowledge of man and his past...

---

253 Ludwig Feuerbach (1804–1872), German philosopher, of some importance to Marx's development.

254 "German Ideology"; possibly a general term but note also the book of this name written by Marx and Engels in 1846, only published 1932, which attacks contemporary German philosophers, including Feuerbach.

255 Claude Bernard (1813–1878), French physiologist. Carl Vogt (1817–1895), German scientist and philosopher. Target of Marx's polemic *Herr Vogt* (1860). Jacob Moleschott (1822–1893), Dutch physiologist. Ludwig Büchner (1824–1899), German physiologist and philosopher, and important figure in the German freethought movement.

256 Probably a typographically incorrect reference to Edward Burnett Tylor (1832–1917), English anthropologist who published *Primitive Culture* in 1871 and *Anthropology* in 1881.

257 Auguste Comte (1798–1857), French philosopher, formulated the idea of positivism, had an important impact on the development of Sociology. From 1817 to 1824 he was Saint Simon's secretary.

Marx of course, expended a gigantic personal effort to which it would be unjust to deny the qualification "scientific." He followed the path that had been laid out conjointly by the economists and the historians, (especially the French historians, Thierry, Guizot, Mignet[258]) who strove to document the rise of the bourgeoisie and the history of the French and British Revolutions. The author of *Capital* applied himself to the most conscientious study of what the economists had turned up on the subject of the modern economic mechanism, and what fairly copious historical sources had revealed about the birth and evolution of capitalist society. Unquestionably the superiority of *Capital* is due to his mastery in these two fields, each of which was enough to tax the efforts of specialists. Nevertheless, the historical portion of *Capital* is not less misleading than Taine's *Origin of Contemporary France*, and the extraordinary precision of the multiplicity of facts, does not keep the image of the "whole" which surges from their connection, from being tendentious, unilateral, and in the last analysis, quite contestable...

But let us ask in what circumstances, in what "situation," has the attempt been made to apply the notion of "objective" science, to the narration (and prediction) of the vicissitudes of human society? To me it seems clear that this kind of endeavor has been peculiar to men endowed with uncommon intelligence who have seen the predictions of their contemporaries, as well as the relationships generally assumed to hold between "intentions" and "results obtained," brutally upset or transcended by events.

The human mind resents upsetting surprises, and strives to assure its coherence at any cost. Thucydides[259], contemplating the unprecedented 30 years war[260] between the two powers that wanted (each in its fashion) a stable and prosperous equilibrium of the Hellenic world, never missed an opportunity to denounce the puerility of the "beautiful tales" in which Herodotus delighted, poking fun on every occasion at the latter's

---

258 Augustin Thierry (1795–1856) French historian. Originally a follower of Saint-Simon, but subsequently developed his own approach. François Guizot (1787–1874), French historian and politician. Prime Minister of France from Sept. 1847–Feb. 1848, after which he left politics. François Mignet (1796–1884), French historian and journalist.

259 Thucydides (c. 460–c. 400 BCE), Greek historian and general.

260 The Peloponnesian War between Sparta and Athens, (431–404 BCE). Thucydides wrote the *History of the Peloponnesian War.*

"providential" conception of the destiny of individuals and of nations. Polybius[261] seeing the series of catastrophes which liquidated the heritage of Alexander[262], spoke with scorn of the "tale-spinning historians" (like Timeus[263] and Philochorus[264]) and tried to show in every event a chain (with no link missing) of "natural" causes, operating independently of the wills, the avowed or secret intentions, the "moral principles" of the protagonists.

Macchiavelli (*sic*) and Guicciardini[265] fall into the same posture—on the subject of the "unexpected" fate of Italy and of Europe—against the whole tradition of Christian historiography and the "anecdotism" of the chroniclers.

These two Italians, like the two Greeks, were concerned to explain the events which had dismayed their contemporaries, and to do so without falling back on the gratuitous hypothesis of a "divine plan," of a preordained end, of any relation whatever between the values venerated by the human mind and the real tribulations of humanity. They wanted to understand their situation in terms of "evident" realities: the human passions and the varying capacities of men (like the *virtù*[266] which enabled a man to dominate and govern his fellows). In the quite restricted limits of these oscillations of quality, the realities and the possibilities of human nature and of society (strictly conditioned by that nature) had always been the same, and it seemed important (from the point of view of men who wanted to preserve themselves from any illusion) to demonstrate that the most extraordinary adventures were part and parcel of "the regular and necessary course of things," and that the plans and prospects of Lycurgus

---

261 Polyibius (c. 200–c. 118 BCE), Greek historian.

262 Presumably Alexander III, king of Macedon, a Greek Kingdom, known as Alexander the Great (356–323), creator by war of a large Empire stretching from Greece to India.

263 Typographically incorrect reference to Timaeus of Tauromenium (c. 356/350–260 BCE), Greek historian.

264 Philochorus (c. 340–c. 261 BCE), Greek historian.

265 Niccolò Machiavelli (1469–1527), Italian diplomat, philosopher and historian. Francesco Guicciardini (1483–1540), Italian historian and statesman: friend and critic of Machiavelli.

266 A term associated with Machiavelli. It implies the practical qualities that allow someone to control other people and/or events.

and of Solon[267], of Christ and of the Apostles, of the wisest and most powerful of monarchs, could never be the determining cause of a collective experience, and could assert themselves at all only by "compromising" with the ineluctable bent of the human herd, while whatever contradicted or transcended the mean level of collective aspiration and comprehension was condemned to a wholly ephemeral and artificial triumph.

The generation of Hegel and of Saint Simon was in its turn swept up in a storm of events which "changed the face of the world": the Industrial Revolution, the French Revolution, Napoleon. Indeed, the historisophical vision of an uninterrupted and gradual ascent towards Liberty expressed the effort of human reason to bring the prodigious again within the scope of the regular, to link the new to the old, preventing "the superstition of the miraculous" and panic before chaos.

Thucydides and Polybius, like Macchiavelli and Guicciardini, may be termed pessimists because according to them humanity could never escape—no matter how astounding its turns of fortune—an always repeated cycle of greatness and collapse, a succession of more or less tolerable servitudes (monarchy—despotism, aristocracy—oligarchy, democracy—ochlocracy[268], and then back to the starting point). But Hegel and Saint Simon, like their successors for several generations, were entirely won over to the doctrine of *progress*: this belief, despite the scarcely "scientific" quality of the arguments advanced by Herber[269] and Condorcet, imposed itself in irresistible fashion on western minds in the eighteenth century. The paradoxes of Rousseau were merely the theory of progress laden with moral condemnation. But the failure of the aims proclaimed (the Industrial Revolution bringing as much poverty as prosperity, the French Revolution new tyrannies along with political enfranchisement, and the ambiguity of the dramatic parable of the "man

---

267 Lycurgus, the legendary lawgiver of Sparta. Though a historical figure, nothing is known about his life or indeed when he lived. Solon, (c. 630–c. 560 BCE), Greek lawmaker credited as a key figure in Athens' move away from the harshness of Draco's law and constitution to democracy.

268 A term for mob rule, which may have been originated by Polybius.

269 Presumably typographically incorrect reference to Johann Gottfried Herder (1744–1803), German philosopher, theologian and writer.

of destiny" as Napoleon appeared to Hegel at Jena[270]), raised between the "mythological" or "anthropomorphic" conception of history and the conception which wanted to be rational, the same conflict that had opposed Thucydides to Herodotus and Macchiavelli to Dante.[271]

It was taken for granted that all humanity was moving towards a "higher level" of material well-being and civilization. But it seemed foolish as well as dangerous to attribute this progress to individual initiatives or to believe that it could be accelerated (or achieved at one stroke) by some wonderful system of abstract invention; it is to be remarked that the Utopians forbade any recourse to "artifices." they (*sic*)[272] demanded, on the contrary, the abolition of the "artificial barriers" raised by despotism, superstition, and the tyranny of traditional manners, calling for a "return" to all that was natural and spontaneous. The charge of violent procedures, aiming at a transformation of human relations in accordance with some "ideology' (*sic*) was merited only by the Jacobins and reformers like Peter the Great[273]; (had Hegel not been the loyal servant of Frederic William III[274], he might perhaps have recognized this "anti-historical" spirit of coercion in the methods of the Prussian government). The actions of men were governed by circumstances rather than "ideas." And there was always a discordance between what a man was "really" (though the problem of affirming and knowing this reality led to inextricable difficulties) and what he believed he was or would have liked to be. (On this point Proudhon does not agree: he conceives of an individual *modestly* certain of what he is and is worth.) The results of each action (with its unforeseeable repercussions) could never coincide with the aim that motivated it, and along with the end achieved or missed innumerable effects could not be prevented from arising, or conceived in all their scope. If one eliminated the hypothesis of a superior will moving men

---

270 Hegel witnessed Napoleon's entry to Jena, a city in Germany, when it was occupied by the French in 1806.

271 Dante Alighieri (1256–1321), Italian poet, notably author of the *Divine Comedy.*

272 Either the full stop at 'artifices' should be a comma, or the t in 'they' should be upper case.

273 Peter 1, known as "the Great" (1672–1725), Czar of Russia who reigned 1682–death, reigning jointly with his brother Ivan until 1696.

274 Frederick William III (1770–1840), King of Prussia who reigned 1797–1840.

about like pawns, it was necessary to seek the significance of events and that which determined their succession in something which would be *at the same time* entirely included within human existence and yet in some way "outside" of man's conscious thought: transcending the horizon of what he knew or willed. The "*Tyche*" [275] of Polybius, like the "*Idea*" of Hegel, merely expressed this "objective" and unfathomably mysterious reality which would be at once "in" men and "above" them, existing only through them (in their consciousness and interactions) but nevertheless determining situations which none of them would have been able to foresee or propose. Materialist views tried to locate these determining factors in nature (climate, race) or in the "things" that men, often without knowing how, had created, but which, persisting, dominated them, imposing on them a regular machinery of gestures, needs, attitudes and styles of life: the division of labor, the reproduction and augmentation of objects necessary for life, institutions of all sorts. Up to the naive pun of Feuerbach: *Mann ist was er isst.*[276]

It is easy for the sceptic to point up the evident insufficiency and unverifiable character of such explanations, the sterile tautology of these formulas, which, in order to avoid the error of defining the whole by a part, limited themselves to merely naming a very complex kernel of definite experiences and obscure intuitions. Science can analyze endlessly our experience of "social reality" and "historical becoming" (in process or past); the problem of a "synthetic" comprehension which would be also an absolete (*sic*)[277] comprehension does not fall within the domain of science, and the intelligence reaches this point only through the flashes momentarily projected in artistic inspiration, metaphysical wonder, the many-colored symbolism of mythology, mystical experience.

---

275 Tyche, Goddess of Fortune in Greek mythology. Polybius was of the view that if no cause of events such as a flood, a drought or a political event can be discovered, the event may be attributed to Tyche.
276 This German phrase means literally: Man is what he eats.
277 Evidently a typographical error for 'absolute'.

> *Too holy for the votive son was the fullness*
> *of high teachings and the depth of not tellable feeling*
> *for him to think worthy of them the dryness of signs.*
> *Thought itself cannot take hold of the soul*
> *when, outside time and space, struck with forebodings of eternity,*
> *it forgets itself and again awakes*
> *to consciousness. He who would tell of this,*
> *even if he spoke with the tongue of angels*
> *would feel the incompetence of words.*
> *He shudders at having made mock of the Made Holy*
> *in his thought and in his words: to say seems to sin,*
> *and trembling he holds his tongue.*
> *This, which the consecrated one forbids himself*
> *is imposed on poorer spirits by a wise law;*
> *not to make known what he in the holy night*
> *has seen and heard and felt.*
> From ELEUSIS the poem Hegel
> dedicated to Hoelderin in August 1796.

The immense power of suggestion which Hegel exercised can be explained by the fact that in his *Phenomenology* as in his lectures on the *Philosophy of History,* he was able to envelope in a "magical" language, (a terminology laboriously intuitive, and laden with chiaroscuros of the densest symbolism), *translations* (or interpretations) in logical form—and hence acceptable to the mind as well as to the emotions—of the truths glimpsed in artistic, mythological or mystical experiences. People believed that it was at last possible to grasp the ineffable by means of discursive thought. Neither Proudhon nor Herzen[278], neither Taine nor Renan, nor many other minds (all exceptionally strong) were able to resist this magical temptation. But these men never lost sight of the fact they had assumed an adventurous (and almost culpable) position, at the crepuscular limits of exact knowledge. In Marx' brief *Notes on*

---

278 Alexander Herzen (1812–1870), Russian revolutionary, immensely influential on Russian populism and agrarian socialism, associated with Pierre-Joseph Proudhon.

Feuerbach[279] there is the outline of a supreme effort to bring back within the circle of positive science these relations between the human being in flesh and blood and the entangled reality of social life. Some people have seen in these Marxist formulas a satisfactory precision. But it seems to me that Marx himself knew he was only on the threshold of insurmountable difficulties, and that he willingly renounced developments which he would perhaps have risked at the time of the *Deutsche Ideologie.*

In any case, we have here a phosphorescent fringe of first principles or ultimate conclusions which the supporters of scientific methods who came after the generation of Marx ("science" as it was understood from 1880 to 1910, to be less vague), simply abstained from exploring.

So it seems to me not quite exact to say the scientific part of Marxism is derived from Hegelian generalizations. Marxist constructions were built against the dogmatic presuppositions of Hegelianism by the critical spirit which distinguished the generation which arrived at intellectual maturity around 1850. Those who more or less explicitly rejected the platitude of empiricism (as Marx did with regard to Bentham), and the abstractness of the classical spirit (criticized by Taine, repudiated by Renan), wanted to safeguard the grand style and vast perspectives of Hegel's spiritual empire, which had been ruined but not duplicated. If I remember rightly, in the preface to *Capital* Marx describes his attachment to certain Hegelian mannerisms as a kind of coquetry stemming from a desire not to fall into the promiscuity of the historians and economists "without ideas," who, parading in eclectic attire, infested the marketplace around 1865—particularly in Germany.[280]

Andrea Caffi

---

279 Presumably the *Theses on Feuerbach,* written by Marx in 1845 as an outline of chapter one of *The German Ideology* (*Deutsche Ideologie,* see above). These, however, were first published in 1888 as a supplement to Friedrich Engels' *Ludwig Feuerbach and the End of Classical German Philosophy.* They take the form of 11 short philosophical notes.

280 In the book Andrea Caffi, *A Critique of Violence,* an alternative translation of this essay can be found as Chapter 12 "Concerning Marx and Marxism", Section 1. "Marx, Science and History", pp. 157–169. The material in this article finishes at p. 163, and at the end on p. 169 the date 1946 is appended.

Machine and Myth[281]

Themes, which I insist on calling "mythological" seem to be intimately bound up with technical inventions from the very beginning, and can scarcely have been absent from the economic and social consequences of these acquisitions in the struggle for the domination of nature. But it would not be impossible to show evidence of the priority of mythological activities even in the domain that Marx studied with most competence: the Industrial Revolution, to which modern capitalism owes its impulse.[282] The period of machine-making did not begin before 1730. But, ever since Leonardo da Vinci, the minds of men in Europe had been haunted by complicated mechanisms possibly moved by natural forces; this can be seen from the numerous fantastic drawings of artists and from semi-scientific, semi-Utopian works. The young Pascal[283] invented machines. All science—particularly since Galileo, who introduced the concepts of mass and acceleration—made a *material* machine of the universe; Descartes even saw machines in animals.... We are wrong to consider the ingenious "epicycles" of Eudoxus and Ptolemy[284] as a dull machinery :

---

281 Article published in *Instead*, no. 3, possibly March 1948.

282 [Caffi's footnote] For the perfecting of implements during the period of manufactures, a fairly brief chapter of Volume 1 of *Capital* yields this very interesting but undeveloped suggestion: That one could demonstrate the successive stages of tool development in a series strongly recalling the affiliation of species as described by Darwin; one tool, better "adapted", replacing "by natural selection" the preceding one, while preserving a kind of kinship with it. This might seem to be the triumphal proof of an almost automatic development, uniquely determined by a dialectic inherent in the material objects themselves. However, there was each time the intervention of the reflection and the will of the man who fashioned the new tool. An object which could not be made without the presence of some skill also seems to require for its production the *contemplation* of some other object. So experiences and impulsions of a "mythological" order cannot be eliminated even from this domain.

283 Blaise Pascal (1623-1662), French mathematician, physicist, inventor and philosopher. It is possible that the machines Caffi is alluding to are his mechanical calculating machines.

284 Eudoxus of Cnidus (c. 390–340 BCE), Greek astronomer and mathematician. Claudius Ptolemy (c. 100–160s/70s), Greco-Roman astronomer and mathematician. In order to make sense of the irregular

Because for the ancients, to whom notions of "force" and of "inertia" could not come into play where the celestial bodies were concerned, these "epicycles" had a geometric virtuosity whose ethereal elegance could scarcely be marred by the complexity of movements uniform, eternal, and harmonious by definition.... It was entirely different after Galileo and Kepler, but most particularly after Newton.... Let us not forget that the making of clocks (which are not means of production), the search for perpetual motion, and the construction of diverting automatons (long before those which made Vaucanson[285] famous) absorbed the minds of inventors before they dreamed of engines for industrial efficiency. Naturally, the Marxist will reply (probably with some condescension) that the "class consciousness" of just-born capitalism was already operating in the direction necessary for the eventual seizure of the controls of the economy. But it would still be necessary to make more precise the steps in the uninterrupted causal series between this hypostatized capitalist demon—which on the one hand was able to push the bourgeois to enrich themselves by trade with India or buying state-functions from the *Roi-Soleil*[286] (Colbert[287] had to use coercion to make them invest their capital in manufactures), and on the other could inspire the intellectuals to dream up the mechanisms which would end by flooding the world markets with junk—and the real individual vicissitudes of Leonardo, Huyghens[288], of Newton, etc. But if these connections are not made, one is always brought back to flat-footed jokes about a suspicious collusion between "mercantile capital" and Shakespeare, and the grain market and Spinoza, jokes less frightening but scarcely wittier than the racist assertion of a necessary relationship between the hooked nose and the practice of usury.

---

movements of planets in their geocentric model of the universe, they derived the now-discarded geometrical concept of "epicycles" to explain them.

285 Jacques de Vaucanson (1709–1782), French inventor. *Instead* used a reproduction of Vaucanson's "Canard Digérant" (Digesting duck), one of his famous automata, as one of the illustrations to Caffi's article. (Another was notably Marcel Duchamp's *The Chocolate Grinder.*)

286 i.e. Louis XIV (1643–1715), King of France.

287 Jean-Baptiste Colbert (1619–1683), First Minister of State of France under Louis XIV.

288 Christiaan Huygens (1629–1695), Dutch mathematician, physicist and inventor.

To arrive at less confused discourse about mythology, or more exactly about the elements of mythological creation, some spontaneous, others deformed by alteration or by artifice (in so far as anti-social powers destroy or corrupt the community), I see that I shall have to wander in a labyrinth without a thread of Ariadne.[289] — In these calamitous times, besides, a thread of the necessary length could be obtained only on the black market... The starting point is given by the *myth of machines* around which revolved the thought of Galileo, Descartes, Leibnitz, and so on, together with the more or less intense sentiments of their contemporaries; let us situate these phenomena in their cultural ambiance, in the fullness of the "baroque"[290] style between the "wars of religion" and the "wars of succession"[291], the theology of the Council of Trent[292] and the quarrels as to whether the folio of Jansenius[293] contained fourteen or one hundred and forty damnable propositions, between the stiff ceremonial of the Escorial and the regal pomp of Versailles.[294] The impressions of a dilettante are enough to evoke the taste for the overloaded, the complicated, the entangled and the mechanical in the art of the period; I am thinking of the machines which multiply in the production of operas, a characteristic delight of the seventeenth century. There are similar traits in the most fashionable novels of the time, including *Don Quixote*.... Of course the term "machine" can correctly be applied to constructions which are not made of wood or iron. Saint Simon[295] quite simply refers to the regularly functioning Court (where everything is enumerated, hierarchized, where all apply themselves to the

---

289 In Greek mythology, Ariadne provided Theseus with a ball of thread so that he could retrace his way out of the labyrinth of the Minotaur.

290 A style of art in Western Europe circa 1600-1750. Uses plentiful ornamentation in decorative arts.

291 The "wars of religion" was a period of wars in Europe in the 16th, 17th and 18th centuries that ended with the Peace of Westphalia, 1648. The "wars of succession" was a period of wars in Europe between the Thirty Years War (1618-1648) and the Coalition Wars (1792-1815).

292 Catholic ecumenical council (1545-1563). Important element of the Catholic response to the Protestant Reformation (the "Counter-Reformation").

293 Cornelius Jansen (1585-1638), Dutch Bishop. His ideas led to the development of the Jansenist movement within Roman Catholicism.

294 Escorial refers to the residence of the King of Spain while Versailles refers to the residence of the King of France.

295 In this case, Louis de Rouvray, duc de Saint-Simon (1675-1755). His memoirs record the Court of Louis XIV at Versailles.

repetition of the same gestures), as "the royal machine". The "invincible Spanish infantry" of Consalvo de Cordova, the army of Wallenstein, the military organization created by Louvois and Vauban[296] are certainly mechanisms. Similarly with the beaurocracies (*sic*) of great centralized and autocratic states. So too with the Roman Church crystallized by the Counter-Reformation and, inside that Church, the Jesuit Order[297].... It would be difficult to show that all this was modeled on the system of manufactures. But within the domain of economic life there was in full swing — and with a force incessant and implacable enough to be set going by the Cartesian vortices — a superlatively rational and automatic system: the circulation of money, which determined the high and low of all individual existence, as of the fortunes of nations. It has become almost a platitude to connect the "reign of money", thanks to which a mobile and abstract wealth (consisting in the possession of the general counterpart of all possible goods, of all joys and of all honors) indefinitely augmentable and transformable, became the nerve of war and peace and, fatally, the sole "measure" of man, with individualism, *Realpolitik*, a conception of the world which reduced every quality to quantitative formulas, a more and more definite bent towards "relativism" in metaphysics and in morals. A very vehement expression of the convergence of these modes of thinking, feeling and living is found in the Elizabethan dramas.... However, I will allow myself to peer further back into the past, not in order to accumulate historical facts, which would be simply boring, but because the phenomena of human societies (and of the mythology which is inherent in them), are best explained when one examines them at their point of origin, at the moment when they first show themselves.

Antiquity also knew the omnipotence of money, the great machine of the absolute state, the intoxication and anguish of individualism, relativism, etc., and even, with an expanding scientific rationalism, came to know forms of "baroque" art and to develop a certain taste for mechanical

---

296 Gonzalo Fernández de Córdoba (1453–1515), Spanish general. Albrecht von Wallenstein (1583–1634), Bohemian military leader on the Catholic side of the Thirty Years War. François-Michel le Tellier, Marquis de Louvois (1641–1691), French Secretary for War under Louis XIV. Sébastien Le Prestre, Marquis of Vauban (1633–1707), French army officer and engineer under Louis XIV.

297 Society of Jesus, a religious order of Roman Catholic clerics founded in 1540 by St. Ignatius of Loyola, with the approval of Pope Paul III.

engines. Michelet[298] cursed Alexander for having imposed on the civilized world the "royal machine". The Macedonian in fact introduced into the Hellenic world something it was never able to eliminate. He had not invented it however, since the essential elements already existed in the monarchy of the Achemaenians[299] as Herodotus has described them. And Cyrus and Darius[300] also found models to hand to copy or to perfect: Assyria[301], for the military mechanism; for the administration and finance, they had the best organized satrapies formed previously in the Lydian kingdom of Croesus.[302] And the tales of the "father of history" have rendered proverbial the association of this name with an almost inexhaustible treasure and magnificent distributions of "buying power"; besides it is to the Lydians that is attributed the invention of coins.

In time the conquest of Alexander had as its principal effect, the putting into circulation of countless talents of gold and silver amassed in Persepolis and Ecbatan.[303] The establishment of Hellenistic autocracy (of which the empire of the Roman Caesars would be only a more brutal continuation) had as a corollary a style of life and esthetic tastes which historians of art have often compared to the modes of baroque art (I should however except certain exquisite aspects of Alexandrian art which might be compared with "Rococo"[304] and with poetic trends for which the

---

298 Jules Michelet (1798–1874), French historian.

299 Achaemenid Empire, an ancient Persian Empire founded by Cyrus in 550 BCE. At the time of Darius III it was conquered by Alexander the Great, in 330 BCE.

300 Cyrus II of Persia, also known as the Great (c. 600–c. 530 BCE), founder of the Achaemenid Empire. Probably Darius I, also known as the Great (c. 550–486 BCE), third ruler of the Achaemenid Empire. Rules the empire at the point of its largest territorial extent.

301 Assyria: a city state that existed from around c. 2025 BCE, becoming an empire in the fourteenth century, until it was conquered around 609 BCE.

302 Lydia; an Iron age kingdom in Anatolia, that became an administrative province of the Achaemenid Empire in c. 546 BCE. Croesus, king of Lydia from c. 585–c. 546 BCE, when Lydia was defeated by Cyrus the Great. His name became synonymous with great wealth.

303 Persepolis: ceremonial capital of the Achaemenid Empire. Ecbatana: ancient capital of the Median kingdom, later summer capital of Achaemenid and Parthian Empires. Possibly located in the Zagros mountains.

304 Rococo: an artistic form prevalent between around 1730 and 1760, sometimes called Late Baroque. Characterised by exceptionally ornamental and dramatic styles.

term "Romanticism" would be more apt). Certainly the infatuation of Westerners of the 17th and 18th centuries with a work like the *Laocoon*[305] shows significant affinities. And from the *Alexandra* of Lycophron[306] to Lucian's *Pharsalia*[307] how many involved "conceits", solemn bombast of artificial contrast, of which Maurice Sceve[308] and the Eupnuists[309], Camoens and Tasso, Gongora and Marino[310] have given us the equivalent. And Michelet insists that Pyrrho[311] and his too radical doubt represented a movement of hopeless revolt of Greek thought against the work of Alexander; the cosmopolitanism of Zeno and the detachment from all participation in the greatness and servitude of the state preached by Epicurus[312], were no less pertinent reactions. From Eratosthenes to Hipparchus[313] the development of Alexandrian science is in many respects comparable to the progress in exact knowledge (even to the relations between scientists and princes) during the century between Bacon and Newton. The formidable siege machines invented by the engineers in the service of Demètrios and Poliorcetes[314], the construction of galleys in which the number of bridges and or superposed rowers reached its point of unwieldiness, the celebrated lenses of Archimedes[315],

---

305 Statue of Laocöon and his sons, excavated in 1506 and put on display in the Vatican Museums.

306 Lycophron (Born c. 330 BCE), Greek tragic poet, to whom the poem *Alexandra* is attributed.

307 A reference presumably to the poem *Pharsalia* (an epic poem about the struggle between Julius Caesar and the Senate led by Pompey the Great), written by Lucan (c. 39–c. 65 CE), a Roman poet born in what is today Spain.

308 Maurice Scève (c. 1501–c. 1564), French poet.

309 Probably a reference to Euphuism, a literary style popular in the Elizabethean era.

310 Luís de Camões (c. 1524–1580), Portuguese poet. Torquato Tasso (1544–1595), Italian poet. Luis de Góngora (1561–1627), Spanish Baroque poet. Giambattista Marino (1569–1625), Italian poet.

311 Pyrrho of Elis (c. 360–c. 270 BCE) Greek skeptic philosopher.

312 Zeno of Elea (c. 490–c. 430 BCE), Greek pre-Socratic philosopher, born in Southern Italy. Epicurus (341–270 BCE), Greek philosopher.

313 Eratosthenes of Cyrene (c. 276–c. 195/4 BCE), Greek polymath born in Libya, chief librarian at the Library of Alexandria. Hipparchus (c. 190–c. 120 BCE), Greek astronomer and mathematician born in Turkey.

314 This appears to be a typographical error, and probably refers to Demetrius I Poliorcetes—which means Demetrius, the besieger of cities—(337–283 BCE), a Greek King.

315 Archimedes (c. 287–c. 212 BCE), Greek mathematician and physicist.

etc., serve to illustrate at least in outline the "mechanization" in a strictly technical sense during the first Hellenic age.

([316]These notes are discontinuous, I would not like to set up parables á la Spengler[317] which can be called suggestive only because they scarcely touch the surface of different historic periods. I would like to try—using certain comparisons only as images—to mark off more precisely the similarity between these two disparate ages: the four or five generations from the death of Plato to the conquest of Greece by the Romans on the one hand, and on the other the three or four generations of "European society" from the world of Shakespeare, Montaigne, Cervantes[318] to the wholly new conditions of social life and the new dominant caste of mind represented by the French libertines, rationalists like Locke, the hegemony of Britain, the advent of Russia and Prussia, Watteau and Defoe.[319] It then seems to me necessary to define less summarily those "mechanisms" whose working is expressed in the "reign of money", individualism, the power politics of centralized states, the conflicts of metaphysics and morality, seeking their foundations in reason and in quantitative determination, etc., to go back further still to the first repercussions of these technical inventions on the collective life of civilized peoples and on the consciousness of men who can be called representative because they have left personal works. Then only would I have some chance of showing what I mean by *spontaneous mythology* (linked to customs and tradition), *evolving mythology* (in the domain that I call "society" *par excellence*), *authentic mythology* (peoples or small groups devoting themselves to the cultivation of intelligence), *false mythology* (deliberately propagated in various ways to obtain definite results) *altered or mutilated mythology* (in the disorder of conditions caused by catastrophe, barbarism, oppression). And then *perhaps* some

---

316 The editor is aware that this parenthesis does not close and is probably a typographical error.

317 Oswald Spengler (1880-1936). German philosopher whose most noted work was *The Decline of the West.*

318 Michel de Montiagne (1533-1592), French philosopher. Miguel de Cervantes (1547-1616), Spanish writer and novelist.

319 John Locke (1632-1704), English philosopher and political theorist. Antoine Watteau (1684-1721), French painter. Daniel Defoe (1660-1731), English writer who wrote *Robinson Crusoe.*

plausible light could be thrown on what is exceptional in the "greek miracle".

ANDREA CAFFI

The Myth and Politics[320]

> "The political parties do not confront each other in terms of what they really are, they oppose each other in terms of myths thanks to which they are able to avoid taking positions which would really separate them."

> Jean Pouillon: *Les Temps modernes*, May 1947.[321]

Ca[322]: See in just what ambiguous fashion the notion of myth is brought into political discussion. For it is clear that if by "myth" Pouillon means not a sheer lie, or some kind of cheating, he in any case thinks it "should not be taken into consideration." He adds, in fact, that "the parties take their desires for realities, but act only on the plane of the imaginary, and limited as they are to symbolic gestures, their effect is one of infantilism." And again: "So it is for their mythologies that we must criticize the political parties, instead of for their monolithic structure or will to power. It is mythology which falsifies all political life."

C.: According to Jean Pouillon, what we have to do is to "unmask" the parties and show what they really are, thus rediscovering the objective significance and value of their action stripped of the halo of "mythologies," which we are to regard as mere camouflages. To bring back clarity into political life would mean, to start with, eliminating the myths which prevent us from seeing the real goals of the political formations, and from evaluating the real effects of their behaviour.

"Mythology falsifies all political life." Apparently, an uncompromising pragmatic rationalism would, contrariwise, clear everything up. In any case, one hypothesis must be excluded: the one which would assert that

---

320 Published in a an undated unpaginated edition of *Instead*, presumably in 1948. Note: all use of italics/bold in original.

321 Jean Pouillon, (1916–2002), French philosopher and anthropologist. Was a member of the editorial board of *Les Temps modernes*, from which this quote was taken, from 1945. The journal was founded in 1945 by Jean-Paul Sartre, Simone de Beauvoir and Maurice Merleau-Ponty, and was an institution on the intellectual left in France until its end in 2019.

322 This is a conversation, as noted at the bottom of the article. "Ca" is Andrea Caffi, and "C." is Nicola Chiaromonte.

it is precisely the monolithic structure, and the will to power, of the parties which causes them to avoid the issues that really separate them.

What exactly does Jean Pouillon refuse to admit? He will not grant that there can be any falsity in the "realism" which obliges the present parties to consider it politically fruitful (or in any case necessary) to act as if there were no contradiction in continually denying by their deeds what they proclaim in discourse, or lead their cleverest followers to read between the lines of their propaganda. To persist in this endeavor, the parties have no recourse but to explain their contradictions away by appealing to precisely what Jean Pouillon calls "myth." To realise the supreme goals of socialism or communism, it seems necessary to contradict them (in appearance, of course) or to disregard them in practice, **_acting as if one were someone else_**. The "myth" embarrasses, and only political blockheads would act in accordance with what it seems to require. But at the same time, it has to be jealously guarded backstage, for without the "myth" nothing of what is done would make sense.

From this, we see that in the "myth" there is something more than an error or a lie; it is actually a political necessity. So much so that one could maintain that the need to "avoid taking positions," is of vital import to the parties as they are today, being an inevitable requirement of a "will to power" that is as empty as you please, but most monolithic.

Ca: In any case, one could show, precisely on the example that Jean Pouillon gives in the course of his article: the Indochinese question, that it is not "myth" but the absence of myth which creates the effect of empty play in the present French parliamentary machinery.

It is quite true that in the discussion about Indochina[323] the partisans of strong-arm methods do not dare to carry to its extreme the principle of power politics (they no longer believe in the myth of the Nation and of the Empire.) And it is also true that the communists do not dare to go beyond their verbal support of the Indochinese. But what is the meaning of this ambiguity? It is that there does not exist among the communists today a mythology like that which the old socialism had created, like that

---

323 Note that the conversation that this article reported took place in June 1947, around sixth months into the French-Indochina War which lasted until July 1954. Effectively, this resulted—following the battle of Dien Bien Phu in Spring 1954—in the defeat of France.

which even the bolsheviks adopted at Baku in 1920[324], a mythology requiring support of colonial peoples; an attitude in which a complete *image of the world* "such as it is and such as it ought to be" implied at the same time an *idea* and an always present *sentiment*, the idea and the sentiment that the Indochinese, the Hindus, the Negroes should, at whatever cost, revolt.

Of course, it was a question not of an equalitarian *ideology*, but of a coherent network of ever-felt representations of "what really is" as contrasted with all the artificiality of a badly ordered existence. In such a felt image, "fraternity with the oppressed peoples" appeared as a simple, and in some way secondary consequence, one in any case beyond discussion. It was not a question of wishful thinking or of ideological construction, and what was "imaginary" or "mythical" in the socialist experience of the nineteenth century, was not inconsistent revery but imagination giving concreteness to something which is more definite and more important than the existence which passes away in time, or the direction of the moment.

Dickens as well as Tolstoi, romantics and rebels who took a stand of moral or esthetic protest against the ugliness and the disorder of modern life, contributed to the formation of this substance of myth which, in turn, affected every intellectual attitude.

On the other hand, if we compare the speeches of Paul Reynaud or Marius Moutet[325] with the myth of *the white man's burden* or of *France's mission*, notions which Kipling[326] and Lyautey came by naturally (The

---

324 A reference to the Comintern organised Congress of the Peoples of the East, held at Baku, Azerbaijan (then part of the Soviet Union) in September 1920.

325 Paul Reynaud (1878–1966), right wing politician, Prime Minister of France, March–June 1940, subsequently arrested by the Vichy regime and then imprisoned by German forces. Played a political role on right of French politics after World War 2. Marius Moutet (1876–1968), French socialist diplomat and politician, Minister of the Colonies 1936-1938, Minster of the Overseas, Jan–Dec 1946. As a socialist deputy he opposed, as one of "the Eighty", the effective dissolution of the French Republic into the Vichy state and went underground to avoid arrest. Apparently favoured independence for Vietnam.

326 Rudyard Kipling (1865–1936), English writer, notable for his poetry. Wrote a poem called "The White Man's Burden" in 1899 in support of American conquest of the Philippines.

myth of France's Mission De Gaulle still holds) we see among the reactionaries and the nationalists of the present day the same absence of myth which is found on the left. The absence of myth on both sides is felt as an absence of reality. Without myth struggles of interest are felt to be empty. At most, we could imagine local and momentary conflicts in which nothing more than utility was at stake. But even a long conflict between two rival families will weave into its substance a variety of images, exaggerations, legends, and so on, which will almost completely cover the real object of the quarrel. Serious international conflicts have always required, to be begun, but more particularly to be continued, a whole mythological apparatus creating an image of oneself as of the enemy. Today, a bad conscience makes it necessary that ideologies be called upon, but the Athenian did not need an ideology to detest the Spartan.

What is needed so that there be myth is: 1) a collective acceptance of an enormous supplement of imaginary things to the reality of everyday existence; 2) that this coefficient of the imaginary penetrate almost every conscious moment, the moment when one ***thinks*** about the things of this world; 3) that the imaginary take coherent forms, capable of developments that are both free and determined, like the developments of a style or of a language—***spontaneous but not arbitrary***.

(A conversation in Toulouse, June 1947, between Chiaromonte and Caffi.)

In Today's Newspaper:[327]

MANCHESTER—The body of a young woman, beaten to death with a hammer, was found by two schoolboys who had been playing in the ruins of bombed houses, less than a hundred yards from the police station.

On the body, two identity cards were found. Under her coat, the victim wore two dresses, two brassieres, two panties, etc. It has been found that she led a double life, alternately in Birmingham and in Manchester.[328]

Think of the quantity of such inexplicable details in each battle, each riot, each day of panic or boom at the Stock Exchange.

Now, the "news item" and the anecdote (i.e., the "other" side of events, great and small) seem to me to be the very substance of history. Any distinction between facts that are "historically important," and those which do not merit this qualification, is arbitrary and absurd, implying a premeditated ignorance of realities that are there just the same. The need to know, the "wonder" which created history as a province of our theoretical conquest of the world, is an attitude of the mind distinct from those which have given rise to magic, scientific knowledge, metaphysical speculation. Doubtless, all these can be found inseparably entwined in mythological creation. But even the primitives studied by Malinowski[329] separate into distinct **genres**, the sacred tales (about the gods, the origin of things, the institution of ritual observances, etc.); the "true" stories about ancestors or far countries, and the "stories invented to amuse ourselves." The overlapping of exact memory and of legend (as of critical exactitude and metaphysical imagination in every science, and of the useful and the ornamental in every craft) are inevitable, since each one of the aspects in which we try to give **form** to our experience embraces that experience in its totality.

There is nothing of all we can know of the world, and of our conscious life in it, which does not fall under the rubric of history. Cosmogony, geology, the development of vegetable and animal species can be fitted

---

327 Published in a an undated unpaginated edition of *Instead*, presumably in 1948. Note: all use of italics/bold in original.

328 This account gives some of the details connected with a notorious case in Manchester, England, in October 1946, the murder of Olive Balchin.

329 Bronislaw Malinowski (1884–1942), Polish anthropologist and ethnologist. Taught at the London School of Economics and Yale University. Main work: *Argonauts of the Western Pacific* (1922).

without arbitrariness into the same series with the annals of all human collectivities that have lived (so can the destinies of the things—buildings, tools, objects of consumption, etc.—fashioned by men). Thus, to turn around the celebrated hypothesis of Laplace[330], it seems permissible to conceive, side by side with the omniscience condensed in a gigantic mathematical formula (positions and relations of everything that existed, exists or will exist in space-time), of a "memory" woven of nothing but qualitative moments instead of quantitative coordinates, and capable of evoking the peculiar vicissitudes of every atom, and of all the combinations of atoms, in the eternity of the universe. With the contradiction, so insoluble to us, between the reality of the present and the unreality of what is no more or is not yet, as well as between the innumerable possibilities, which are not however just nothing, and all that chance has let be realized.

In limiting historical knowledge to the destinies of man and of human societies we are faced with a groundless disproportion between "what one must know" and the few fragments we know with "certainty." Nothing comparable to what physicists, chemists, and so on, can anticipate in the way of more exhaustive analysis and experiments, for example, to fill in the gaps of Mendeleiev's[331] table of elements, or to verify the calculation of Einstein with respect to the orbit of the planets. But historians can argue on the other hand that the slightest fact they succeed in bringing to light is intrinsically valuable. I here consciously pit myself against a school of thinking which is scarcely challenged nowadays; a school which is prepared to respond to a fact only if it clarifies some group of facts or suggests ingenious analogies that lead to the discovery of other classes of facts. From my point of view, history is the memory of our past: this past interests us **as such** in its most futile details, and shapes itself in our consciousness purely as the recollection of existences which persevere in us. By the same token, I would reject any confusion, **a la** Hegel or Croce, of historical knowledge with philosophical knowledge. History is a particular mode, neither mathematico-scientific nor metaphysico-scientific, of knowing the human world.

---

330 Pierre-Simon, Marquis de Laplace (1749–1827), French polymath. His deterministic hypothesis, known as Laplace's demon, was that if someone knew the exact position and motion of every particle, and knew all the laws of nature, they could then calculate the universe's entire past and future.
331 Dmitri Mendeleev (1834–1907), Russian chemist, originator of the periodic table of elements.

Of course, the overlapping of the various modes of knowledge is inescapable. In studying the acceleration of a ball on an inclined plane, the physicist has to tell the "story" of this movement, and even the solution of an equation with x unknowns can be described as a "development," hence a historical phenomenon. Since antiquity, men have not left off composing "histories" of animals along with natural histories. Discourse is always a "recital." On the other hand, the philosopher, like the historian, ought to "know everything." One can scarcely imagine a historian of some mettle who does not have a more or less encyclopaedic knowledge, and who is not only a keen psychologist but also sufficiently skilled in philosophy to understand the ideologies expressed or carried out by the characters he describes. But all these necessary distinctions are valuable on the condition that, as the historian Marc Bloch[332] said, "one is not their dupe."

ANDREA CAFFI

---

332 Marc Bloch (1886–1944), French historian. Founder of the *Annales* school of history. Involved during the occupation in the resistance, he was captured by the Gestapo and summarily executed in 1944.

Mass Politics and the Pax Americana[333]

By ANDREA CAFFI

Addressing himself to what he calls "the Babbits[334] of the Left," Arthur Koestler[335] has tried to convince them that "either there will be in the world a *Pax Americana*, or there will be no peace at all"; and that, faced with the struggle between Stalinist absolute "black" and American "grey," it would be frivolous to insist on looking for "the perfect cause": any sensible person must *choose* the relatively good side represented by official American policies, Truman's "grey" cause.

✳   ✳   ✳   ✳   ✳

Koestler warns us, in his superior way, that "to live and die for a perfect cause is a luxury granted to few." Hence, he summons the Babbits of the Left to enlist in the great anticommunist army. "Russian totalitarianism," he says, "is black: its victory would spell the end of our civilization... American democracy is not white, but grey."

We would indeed be ready not to be fussy, to accept a "half truth" in order not to be lost in a "total lie" (even though from a purely logical point of view it is very hard to imagine such an adhesion of the mind to a "truth" which *is known* to be half "false"). Koestler himself, however, has sown

---

333 First published as an appendix of sorts in Dwight Macdonald, *The Root is Man*, 1953. Macdonald notes that the article had been sent in too late for the final edition of *politics* (which appeared as the "Winter 1949" edition. In line with American practice, this probably appeared in early 1949.) The 1995 Semiotext(e) edition of this book—which appears to still be in print—does not contain Caffi's essay. Marco Bresciani indicates that this essay was a version of a piece contributed by Caffi to the Italian journal *Critica Sociale* in November 1948, and called "I ragionamenti di Koestler". M. Bresciani, *La rivoluzione perduta*, Bologna, p. 287, footnote 135.

334 Presumably a reference by Koestler to Sinclair Lewis's 1922 novel, *Babbitt*. Koestler, Caffi or Macdonald have misspelt the title of the book. Based on the novel, the term came to mean someone who holds conventional opinions.

335 Arthur Koestler, (1905-1983). Koestler, among other things, had been a Communist between 1931 and 1938. Following his leaving the Communist movement he became a notable anti-Communist in the polemics of the Cold War era.

more than a little doubt in our minds by talking, a little earlier in his speech[336], about "Error Number Seven," namely "soulsearching." To the "soul-searchers" of 1939–1940 he attributes the following fallacy: "We have no right to *fight* Hitler's plans for the extermination of *six million Jews* as long as, in America, the Negroes will not enjoy absolute equality with the whites."

Now, as far as Hitler and us Babbits of the Left are concerned, two things are sadly certain: the first is that six million Jews did actually die in the gas chambers, in the Warsaw ghetto, and elsewhere, the second is that it didn't make the slightest difference whether we, the Babbits of the Left, did or did not *fight* Hitler's plans. Those who could have saved at least a part of those victims by giving them immigration visas didn't do anything. Hitler went ahead. Was it because we Babbits of the Left wasted time "soulsearching," or looking for "the perfect cause"? Or rather because the inexorable procedure of the struggle between "grey" and "black" consisted in, first, letting the hangmen do their work; second, adding to the flood of their nefariousness the devastations of a total war, and finally avenging the memory of innumerable victims in the indeed "grey" assizes of Nuremberg and Tokyo[337]?

In the same way, whatever the decisions or hesitations of the Babbits of the Left, the fact remains that the future struggle against communism will have had, as a first phase, the agreements of Tehran, Yalta and Potsdam[338], by which the peoples of Poland, Czechoslovakia, Rumania, etc. (hence the individual destinies of the various Petkovs, Manius, and Masaryks[339])

---

336 The speech seems to be one reproduced in Koestler's *Bricks to Babel* as "The Seven Deadly Fallacies", given in Spring 1948 at Carnegie Hall, New York, or a variant of that speech. In that version, "soulsearching" is 'the second fallacy'. A. Koestler, *Bricks to Babel,* New York, Random House, 1980, pp. 240–241 for this material.

337 The trials regarding Nazi war crimes at Nuremburg (Nov. 1945–Oct. 1946), and regarding Japanese war crimes at Tokyo (Apr. 1946).

338 The Teheran Conference, 1943, the Yalta Conference, February 1945, and the Potsdam Conference, July/August 1945. Three meetings of the Allied "Big Three" – i.e. the UK, USA and USSR- leaders during the Second World War.

339 Nikola Petkov (1893–1947), politician, leader of the Bulgarian Agrarian National Union, executed by the Bulgarian Communist regime in 1947. Presumably Iuliu Maniu (1873–1953), politician, leader of Rumanian National Peasants Party, arrested and imprisoned by Rumanian Communist regime after a show trial and died in prison in 1953. Jan Masyryk (1886–1948), Czech

have been explicitly abandoned to Stalin's unmerciful hand. The second phase will be the release of rockets, atom bombs, superpoisons, etc., all over the world, while underneath will rage the most chaotic of all civil wars. At the end, the hypothetical survivors will celebrate this triumph of civilization, or rather: of "half-civilization," over black barbarism.

In his great work on contemporary history, Polybius of Megalopolis showed his Hellenic countrymen that the only reasonable "choice" was a resigned acceptance of the *Pax Romana* all over the Mediterranean world. He deemed it useless to add any consideration on the "black" and the "grey," on "half-truths" and "total lies," since he wasn't trying to minimize, or to get away from, an ineluctable situation caused by an accumulation of human errors, but also by those blows of Fortune against which no human will can prevail.

Polybius didn't pretend to believe that the destruction of Carthage and Corinth, and the subjection of all the Greek communities to the greed of proconsuls and publicans, were ways of "saving civilization." If, in spite of the scourges which devastated Greece and the Hellenistic world for more than one century after Polybius' death, Greek civilization didn't perish altogether, this was due to the inconspicuous work carried on almost "underground" (but in any case far from the spectacular machinations of "mass action" and "global" politics) by persisting communities: religious sects; humble "municipia" like Plutarch's[340] Cheronea; artisans' brotherhoods; associations of mutual help between people of the same town or of the same religion. Something of Greek civilization survived because the passion to "educate," to transmit and propagate a certain heritage of "superior humanity," never died out.

As long as today's problems are stated in terms of "mass politics" and "mass organization," it is clear that only States and mass parties can deal

---

diplomat and politician, found dead 10th March 1948, in the courtyard of the Czechoslovak Foreign Ministry. The Czechoslovak Communist government stated that he had committed suicide, a view that has been disputed.
340 Plutarch (C. 40–C. 120s CE), Greek philosopher and historian, born in the small town of Chaeronea, east of Delphi.

with them. But, if the solutions that can be offered by the existing States and parties are acknowledged to be either futile or wicked, or both, then we must look not only for different "solutions" but especially for a different way of stating the problems themselves.

To begin with, it is evident that it doesn't make any sense to worry about "problems" as long as one has the feeling that one cannot "get to the bottom" of anything, and that it is imperative to go on living, to cultivate one's garden, to ingest the daily meal, and to pay one's debts (as George Eliot[341] put it).

There are men and women. As units in a "mass," they submit to uniform rules of housing, eating, and dressing; go to the factory or to the movies; vote for a party or acclaim a Leader. Finally, it is as "masses" that they let themselves be enlisted, drilled, and led to the slaughter for the Fatherland, for democracy, or for civilization. Yet, each one of them has been a child. Each one has made, *by* himself and *for* himself, the discovery of the world and of his own consciousness. Each one, as an adolescent, has experienced "unique" moments of love, friendship, admiration, joy of living or unmotivated sadness. Even in the greyest existences, there are traces of aspiration to a life less debased, to a real communion with one's neighbors. One can hardly imagine a human life without some moments of carefree enjoyment and enthusiasm, or without dreams.

The "mass," however, wouldn't be so ghastly a phenomenon if it didn't also cause the ruthless recourse to egoism; total vulgarity, ferocious and self-satisfied; the "extreme situations" of physical and moral degradation from which there is no way out; the violent escape from the stifling anonymity of mass life into the frenzied attempts to emerge from the crowd, to dominate, to inflict suffering on others, and on oneself.

All this knocks down any faith in a pre-established "human progress," but also shows that the apparent compactness, and smooth working, of "mass existence" hides a frightful precariousness of human situations; that to build on the masses is tantamount to building on quicksand, and that the "collective suicide" of which the Atom Bomb has become the vulgarized symbol and scarecrow, could well be, according to both nature and to

---

341 George Eliot, pseudonym of Mary Ann Evans (1819–1880), English novelist.

reason, the only outcome (a kind of Aristotelian "entelechy") of a "mass civilization" with all the "planning" and the mechanizations that it involves.

Is it possible today to define a "politics of the people" as opposed to mass politics?

In order to be clear about the problem, it is imperative not to forget that the substitution of the "masses" (organized and manoeuvred *as such*) for the people is not a communist invention. As for the Nazis, they only pushed to the extreme consequences of an absolute *efficiency* the methods of political and labor action created by socialdemocracy[342] first in Germany, and then in in all the countries where German socialdemocracy was taken as a model for socialist action. From 1889 to 1914, however, European socialism found its justification in the fact that, in spite of its proclaimed adherence to political "realism," mass tactics, and State worship, the humanitarian utopia and the sense of the immediate realities of communal life were never obliterated. Men like Auguste Bebel, Jaurès, and Turati[343] were too humane and generous to yield without reservations to the logic of the "*raison d'Etat*," that is to say, to those methods of power politics (which are also "mass" methods) which were promptly taken over both by Ebert and Noske[344] and by Lenin's team.

What distinguishes "mass politics" is the fact that it reduces human beings and their occasional spontaneity to the function of undifferentiated and interchangeable particles of energy of which the only thing that matters is how quickly they can be agglomerated into large numbers and "big battalions."

As everybody knows, the Moscow apparatus succeeds in exploiting for the sake of "mass operations" the strongest and noblest qualities of the individual. The consistency, and hence the superior effectiveness, of the

---

342 Caffi is clearly referring to the German Social Democratic Party, SPD.

343 Auguste Bebel (1840–1913), a founder, and leading official of the German Social Democratic Party. Filippo Turati (1857–1932), leading figure in the Italian Socialist Party, and the reformist split from it dating to 1922, the Unitary Socialist Party.

344 Friedrich Ebert (1871–1925) and Gustav Noske (1868–1946), German Social Democratic Party leaders in the period after World War 1.

Communist leadership stems from the fact that it inculcates in the minds subjected to it the explicit conviction that a man has neither existence nor value outside of the mass, and that any contemptible "free will" must be suppressed in favor of a vigorously disciplined unanimity, which the Communists extol as the supreme, and final, state of the human kind.

If the preceding considerations are at all relevant, we must conclude that the first thing to do, in order to get to the point where "politics of the people" will be more than a phrase, is to begin from the beginning, that is: with the rescue of individuals from the mass that mechanizes and dehumanizes them. We must find again the direct language, the genuine feelings, the clear notions, the limpid images through which we can establish a true communication with the "people."

In order to define the "politics of the people" we should, for example, refuse to stop at the surface of the desire for peace which, in the general and vague form exploited, for example, by Wallace[345], is a typical mass phenomenon. We should probe deeply into the cluster of feelings, hopes, altruistic or egocentric dispositions which color, and make more or less consistent the "pacifism" of a particular group or individual.

Rather than solidarity, we should promote friendship among the individuals who struggle to emerge from the "mass." Those friendships should then be strengthened through some constructive enterprise carried out in common. The aim remains the rebirth of true "popular" communities. The humblest aims, from an association for mutual help to a club where people meet to spend time together, can eventually lead to an association whose unwritten norms will actually inspire both the private and the public life of its components. Two conditions are obviously indispensable: the first is that the number of people so associated be limited, so as to permit each individual to get to know *well* all his

---

345 Henry Wallace (1888–1965), US Vice-President 1941–1945, under F. D. Roosevelt. Wallace was the nominee of the Progressive Party in the 1948 presidential election, in which he received 2.4% of the popular vote. The party was perceived as being close to the Communist Party, and Wallace shifted his views on Foreign Affairs and left the party in 1950 at the outbreak of the Korean War.

companions; the second, is that such an association be not made dependent on an authority endowed with means of coercion.

We must wake again in the individual the courage to frankly assert his need for *happiness,* and no longer resign himself to substitutes, conformism and "ideological" imbecility. In Europe, we haven't got empty space to escape to from the suffocation of mass regimes. The only escape open to us is a bold and uncompromising recourse to reason (which, among other things, would mercilessly ridicule any form of authoritarianism, theocracy, "ideocracy," or of what Sartre calls *l'esprit de serieux*[346]) and to a sociability so refined, so vigilant, and so tolerant, as to give the individual, together with a sense of common purpose and solidarity, a feeling of full personal independence.

Only through the reawakening and cultivation of such qualities can we slowly build a "civilization of the people" in opposition to the "civilization" of the masses, where everything tends to be measured in terms of sheer utilitarianism, stability is again and again sought on the lowest possible level, and a coarse pragmatism is supposed to be the measure of all truth and all justice.

(Translated by Nicola Chiaromonte)

---

346 In the "Key to Special Terminology" appended to the English translation of *Being and Nothingness* there is a definition of this term: "Serious. The "Spirit of Seriousness" (*l'esprit de sérieux*) views man as an object and subordinates him to the world. It thinks of values as having an absolute existence independent of human-reality." Jean-Paul Sartre, *Being and Nothingness*, London, Methuen & Co., 1957, p. 633. (Trans. Hazel Barnes).

Afterword

Antifascism and the Critique of Violence: The Power of Andrea Caffi's Ideas

In the Face of World Wars and Totalitarianism

The thirty years of wars and totalitarianisms that began in 1914 and ended with the atomic destruction of the Japanese cities produced in contemporaries a profound disorientation: the categories that, up to 1914, had served to describe the world and to guide decision-making appeared by the mid-1940s entirely obsolete—relics of a world that had by then vanished. The sense of disorientation affected everyone, but it was particularly acute among socialists, who had witnessed the shipwreck of their ideals not only in the war but also in the totalitarian drift of the Soviet Union, which had buried the aims of liberty and justice for which socialism had originally come into being. It was therefore a matter of finding new paths toward socialism, recovering the aims that had given rise to the movement and devising means appropriate to their attainment.

In the United States, among the socialist-oriented intellectuals who undertook this task with depth and intelligence, Dwight Macdonald stands out. Between 1944 and 1947, Macdonald published the journal *politics* (with a lowercase "p"), in whose pages one finds, among other things, elaborate critiques of the Soviet Union and incisive reflections on war, political violence, and socialism.[347] As for war, Macdonald adopted resolutely pacifist positions, reconnecting with the American radical tradition and, in particular, with the ideas that another New York

---

347 About the internal debate within these journals, see J. R. Conlin, "Introduction", in J. R. Conlin (ed), *The American Radical Press. 1880–1960*, Westport, Greenwood Press, 1974, (vol. I), pp. 3–19; and A. Donno, *Dal New Deal alla Guerra fredda. Aspetti del radicalismo statunitense negli anni '40*, Firenze, Sansoni, 1983, pp. 159–183. On the revival of American anarchism and radicalism in the 1940s, see L. Veysey, *The Communal Experience: Anarchist and Mystical Counter-Cultures in America*, New York, Harper and Row, 1973, pp. 37–40. For an account of the aims of *politics*, see Macdonald's first editorial, "Why politics?", *politics*, n. 1 (1944), pp. 6–8.

intellectual, Randolph Bourne[348], had articulated in 1917. In his essay *The War and the Intellectuals,* Bourne deemed absurd the attempts of American intellectuals to legitimize entry into the war in the name of liberty and democracy. In his view, war was the domain of violence, of wild emotions, of fanaticism, and thus any attempt to bend it to some purportedly good reason appeared to him doomed to failure.[349] In 1944, in the editorial of the first issue of *politics,* Macdonald took up Bourne's arguments, asserting that the moral reasons invoked to legitimize the war—even though it was a war against Hitler—were spurious and sophistic, intended only to conceal the stark reality of a conflict in which justice had no place. Thus, if it was true that socialists could not remain passive in the face of the advance of Nazism, it was equally true that the war waged by American capitalism could not represent a desirable solution.[350]

Such radical ideas were, of course, far from predominant in 1940s New York; nevertheless, Macdonald was by no means isolated, and he had interlocutors of considerable stature. Let us recall that, around *politics* and its editor, there gathered figures resistant to every form of conformism and of profound culture such as Mary McCarthy, Paul Goodman, C. Wright Mills, or Hannah Arendt. Yet when Macdonald, through Nicola Chiaromonte, became acquainted with Andrea Caffi's ideas on violence, war, and socialism, he was profoundly struck by them. In a 1947 letter addressed to Chiaromonte, Macdonald referred to an

---

348 (Editorial Footnote): Randolph Bourne (1886-1918), American intellectual and notable opponent of US entry into World War One.

349 R. Bourne, "The War and the Intellectuals", *The Seven Arts,* June 1917, now in R. Bourne, *War and Intellectuals. Collected Essays 1915-1919,* (ed.) C. Resek, New York, Harper and Row, 1964 (second edition Hackett Publishing Company, Indianapolis, 1999), pp. 3-14. Bourne's ideas influenced Macdonald to such an extent that, in 1939, he published an article in *Partisan Review* entitled "War and Intellectuals," leaving no doubt either about who inspired it or about its content. D. Macdonald, "War and Intellectuals. Act Two", *Partisan Review,* n. 6 (1939), pp. 6-8.

350 D. Macdonald, "Why politics?", 8. On these and other topics, in *politics* Macdonald gathered contributions from major American and European writers. He published, for example, essays by Lionel Abel, Albert Camus, Lewis Coser, Nicola Chiaromonte, Paul Goodman, Karl Jaspers, George Orwell, Victor Serge, Simone Weil, George Woodcoock, C. Wright Mills, beside those by Andrea Caffi. See H. Wilford, *The New York Intellectuals. From Vanguard to Institution,* Manchester University Press, Manchester,1995, p. 152.

(unspecified) essay by Caffi as one of the things he was proudest to have published; and when, in 1953, he brought out a new edition of his celebrated essay *The Root is Man,* he placed Caffi's article *Mass Politics and Pax Americana* in the appendix to the volume.[351] What accounted for Macdonald's admiration for an aging, defeated, and isolated European revolutionary like Caffi? What sort of fascination could the ideas of a socialist born in Russia in 1887 exert on an intellectual engaged in rethinking radical thought in the United States in the mid-1940s?

The Nature of Fascism

Throughout his life, Caffi maintained that the aim of socialist action should be the liberation of society from the oppression of every form of power. Caffi wrote that power "does not know any other end nor any other reason for existence but its own perpetuation". It does not "regard the people as anything but an object *taillable à merci*[352] and society (that is, the fabric of spontaneous and creative relations between individuals and groups) as anything but a senseless and irksome obstacle".[353] For him, socialism was the revolt of human spontaneity and of cooperation among equals against any mechanism of regimentation or top-down control. The aim of socialism, then, had to be the creation of the conditions under which spontaneous relations of sociability and friendship could arise and develop among individuals and groups. It is clear that such an aim could not be achieved through coercion: sociability cannot be imposed by force; it must be allowed to grow out of itself, in accordance with its own tradition. Consequently, for Caffi, the development of socialism was incompatible with the exercise of power and with violence in general.

Where does this conception of socialism originate? Caffi's biography is complex and rich in deep resonances: the 1905 Revolution, the influence of writers such as Proudhon, Herzen, Bakunin, Tolstoi and Kropotkin, his study of German sociology, his experience in the trenches of the First World War, Bolshevik Russia, Fascist Italy, and clandestine activism in

---

351 Letter from Macdonald to Chiaromonte, April 7th 1947, see G. D. Sumner, *Dwight Macdonald and the politics Circle: The Challenge of Cosmopolitan Democracy,* p. 260, footnote 70.

352 (Editorial Footnote): "*taillable à merci*": French for endlessly exploitable.

353 A. Caffi, "Society, the "Elite" and Politics", in *A Critique of Violence,* p. 74.

occupied France all contributed to shaping a cultural and psychological fabric whose complexity it is impossible, in the present context, to do full justice to. It is, however, worth making clear at least that an important moment in the development of the ideas that Macdonald would so greatly admire coincided with the period of his antifascist struggle—or, rather, with the search for a form of opposition to Fascism that did not set itself merely the goal of overthrowing the dictatorship, but aimed instead at removing the deeper causes that had made its establishment possible.

Caffi arrived in Rome from the Soviet Union in 1923, and as early as June 1924 he published "Cronaca di dieci giornate" (Chronicle of Ten Days) in the journal *Volontà*. In that essay, analyzing the events that had preceded and followed the murder of the socialist parliamentarian Giacomo Matteotti[354] at the hands of Mussolini's *squadristi*, he dwelt on the origins of the regime. Caffi traced Fascism back to the despair and disorientation into which the war had thrown the masses; that is, Mussolini's success appeared to him to be determined by the political weight of the war veterans "*déclassés*[355], proletarianized men who, having nothing to lose", did not hesitate to support the political force that put forward the emptiest and coarsest slogans.[356] Similar observations were taken up by Caffi the following year, in a short article entitled "Sul tramonto della civiltà europea" (On the Decline of European Civilization), published in *La vita delle nazioni*. With the aim of clarifying where the Spenglerian "decline" of Europe that culminated in Fascism had originated, Caffi gave voice to what he termed an "apocalyptic conception", according to which the "systematic orgy of mechanical rapidities" unleashed upon the European peoples between 1914 and 1918 had annihilated the "creations" and "values" of civilization. According to this "conception", moreover, the "death sentence" of

---

354 (Editorial Footnote): Giacomo Matteotti (1885–1924), Italian Socialist politician and member of the Chamber of Deputies, kidnapped and murdered by the forces of the Mussolini regime in June 1924 following a speech condemning Fascist electoral fraud and violence in the Chamber on 30 May 1924. "*Squadristi*": in this context Fascist Blackshirt paramilitaries acting on behalf of the Mussolini regime.

355 (Editorial Footnote): "*déclassés*": having lost social standing.

356 A. Caffi, "Cronaca di dieci giornate", *Volontà*, 30 giugno 1924; now in G.Landi (ed), *Andrea Caffi un socialista libertario*, (ed. G. Landi), Pisa, Biblioteca Franco Serantini,1996, pp. 186–188.

European civilization was further confirmed, in the postwar period, "by the new tastes of the masses, by the spread of 'standardizing' Americanism, and by the wretched fate of the intellectual classes". Caffi added, finally, that the effects of this crisis had struck a Europe already afflicted by "economic and demographic imbalances", "national fanaticisms", "unjust and unenforceable treaties", and "class antagonisms either too exacerbated or dangerously distorted by [...] institutions no longer vital or by ruling groups neither capable nor worthy".[357]

Seven years after these reflections, in the essay written in Paris and entitled *La dottrina fascista. O il fascismo nella storia superiore del pensiero* (The Fascist Doctrine. Or Fascism in the Higher History of Thought), Caffi once again maintained that the dictatorship arose "not from hidden depths but from the tumult of confused aspirations that stirred the ranks from whom Mussolini sought to exact obedience". They were "ranks" accustomed to violence, to blind obedience in the factory and under arms, to the crudest demagogy, and to the belief that complex problems could be solved through sudden, definitive actions: a "rabble of misfits and unstable individuals", born of an unprecedented, desperate crisis and devoid of any capacity for planning.[358] The irruption of these masses into politics could not correspond to any positive development, but only to the establishment of a new form of tyranny, masked as revolution through the shrewd manipulation of popular moods by unscrupulous leaders. The outcome of all this, only a few years after the Fascist takeover, was "an extension of militarism to every branch of administration and social organization, carried out with a ruthlessness and pushed to extreme consequences to which never before, at least among Western peoples, had a 'warrior' lordship dared to go".[359]

---

357 "Sul tramonto della civiltà europea", *La Vita delle Nazioni*, I, nn. 6–7, October 1925; now in Andrea Caffi, *Scritti politici*, Firenze, La Nuova Italia, 1970, pp. 64–66.

358 A. Caffi, *La dottrina fascista. O il fascismo nella storia superiore del pensiero*, (ed. Alberto Castelli), Milan, Biblion, 2022, p. 8.

359 A. Caffi, *La dottrina fascista*, p. 9.

Putting Back in Order "a world out of joint"

If fascism had therefore been able to assert itself thanks to the despair of the masses, in turn caused by an unprecedented political, social, and economic crisis, what was the remedy? A mere political overturning was certainly not enough to defeat fascism; it was necessary to go deeper and uproot the noxious growth that had produced the poisoned fruit of dictatorship. In the early 1930s, Caffi drew closer to the *Giustizia e Libertà* (Justice and Liberty) movement, led by Carlo Rosselli[360], who had gathered around himself in Paris numerous activists and intellectuals determined to fight Mussolini. Between 1932 and 1935, then, Caffi took part in the discussion on the methods and objectives of the anti-fascist struggle within the movement, writing several essays of considerable importance. For our purposes, it is worth recalling "In margine a due lettere dall'Italia" (About Two Letters from Italy), published in 1934 in the journal *Quaderni di Giustizia e Libertà.*[361] After reiterating that fascism was the result of a profound crisis of European civilization, Caffi stated that an effective anti-fascism would have to consist in an action just as deep. In other words, if fascism was the symptom of a deterioration of Europe's social and moral fabric, the remedy could not be confined to a superficial level. It could not, for example, consist in the mere overthrow of Mussolini's government; it would instead have to concern itself with acting on the deeper causes of the crisis, strengthening social bonds and renewing civil coexistence through a deep and patient work of reconstruction of every aspect of what makes life human.

In this perspective, Caffi argued for the need to oppose fascism with an intellectual and revolutionary elite that would carry out a work of education and formation of consciences capable, in the long run, of overcoming the violence of fascist domination. According to Caffi, there was no lack of examples of the effectiveness of this strategy in history: "The desert of powerless ascetics has defeated the empire of Diocletian (...) the

---

360 (Editorial Footnote): Carlo Rosselli (1889–1937), Italian socialist and antifascist leader, murdered on the orders of the Fascist regime. See: Stanislao G. Pugliese, *Carlo Rosselli, Socialist Heretic and Antifascist Exile,* Cambridge (Mass), Harvard University Press, 1999. As noted in the introduction, M. Bresciani, *Learning from the Enemy,* is a useful English language source on *Giustizia e Libertà.*

361 A. Caffi, "In margine a due lettere dall'Italia", *Quaderni di Giustizia e Libertà* (1934), now in A. Caffi, *Scritti politici,* pp. 165–180.

'underground Russia', that is, a handful of outlaws and 'nobodies', ended up devouring Tsarism, despite the bayonets, the centuries-old prestige, and all the support of Western plutocracy".[362] Caffi also observed that no violent revolution had ever achieved the goal of a true liberation of human beings and that, ultimately, authoritarian reaction has always "cut short the impetus of the popular masses, yearning for a real emancipation". In his view, therefore, a drastic choice was necessary: either definitively abandon "any use of organized violence in relations between human communities", or resign oneself to the impossibility of building a more just and free society.[363]

It may be, however, that the most evocative and significant statement of Caffi's notion of anti-fascism appears not in a work meant for print, but in a letter he sent to Carlo Rosselli on 22 July (probably) 1933. "A movement capable of awakening serious interest in people's consciences must subordinate politics to certain broader spiritual values and frame political action within a comprehensive vision of social engagement (education, economy, customs) [...]. To put back in place 'a world out of joint'[364], it is necessary for an ideology to take shape that is well-represented by genuine 'elites' and sufficiently ingrained in broad segments of society—truly worthy of a pivotal moment in universal history. Thus, an immense effort of critical thinking, indispensable creation, apostolate, and heroic examples are required, the kind inspired by true faith (I don't speak of 'heroic deeds', which naturally have their value, but of the heroism of an entire life). What remains of my life I would dedicate to nothing else than the liberation of Europe: 1 from the deadly encrustations of the pre-war period, 2 from the hideous scum of the war. I believe the two must be destroyed together because one sustains the other; false democracy, plutocracy, communist dictatorship, and fascist dictatorship feed off each other, providing one another with pretexts to appear 'necessary or desirable'".[365] To heal from the moral and civil illness that gave rise to fascism, political activism alone was insufficient; it was necessary to administer a deeply acting cure to the patient. Those who

---

362 A. Caffi, "In margine a due lettere dall'Italia", p. 167.

363 A. Caffi, "In margine a due lettere dall'Italia", p. 171.

364 In English in the original text.

365 A. Caffi "Lettera a Carlo Rosselli", in "Storia in Lombardia", XVI, n. 2, (1996), pp. 165-166. See A. Castelli, *The Peace Discourse in Europe 1900-1945*, pp. 191-204.

wished to take on this task should not have aimed for power, nor should they have used political violence (with all that it entailed); instead, they had to follow their conscience, 'go to the people' with an apostolic mission, study thoroughly, rebuild social life, propose new ideas, and offer radical solutions.

A Strange Idea of Revolution

When, starting in 1944, Macdonald and Chiaromonte urged Caffi to set out his views on socialism and revolution in the pages of *politics*, he reformulated and deepened the ideas he had expressed in the 1930s, in the context of organizing the anti-fascist struggle, eventually developing a fully-fledged critique of political violence. The core of this critique is already contained in the opening sentences of Caffi's most significant essay to appear in *politics*, "Violence and Sociability": "My thesis is that a 'movement' which has its aim assuring men bread, freedom and peace, and that therefore intends to abolish wage labor, the subordination of society to the coercive apparatus of the State (or Super-State), the separation of men in classes as well as in foreign and potential hostile nations, must give up considering as useful or even viable the various means of organized violence, that is: a) armed insurrection; b) civil war; c) international war (even against Hitler ... or Stalin); d) a regime of dictatorship and terror to consolidate the 'the new order'".[366] For Caffi, the resort to these means could only reinforce oppressive structures and result in a denial of the socialist ideal. No war—whether civil or between states—could be won without a well-organized, efficient army built on a hierarchical structure capable of suppressing individual wills and desires and turning people into virtual automatons. Yet the very moment such an army came into being, the struggle ceased to be one of free men against oppression and became instead a confrontation between two armies, each commanded by a ruling caste that exercised oppressive power in comparable ways and compelled its soldiers to fight. The conclusion is that it makes no sense to aim at fostering freedom and justice through war, for placing oneself in a position to win it means automatically renouncing the very ideals for which it was undertaken.

---

366 A. Caffi, "Violence and Sociability", *politics*, (1947) retitled "A Critique of Violence", in *A Critique of Violence*, 1970, p. 35.

Revolution (the struggle for a more humane and civil society), according to Caffi, has nothing to do with the use of arms, with the manipulation of the masses through slogans, or with the shrewd management of power, because these methods lead to new forms of dictatorship. Revolution, by contrast, meant a constant and tireless effort to nurture what is human in each person: to awaken their longing for genuine experience, spontaneous sociability, personal independence, and a life untouched by degradation.

The subject that, according to Caffi, should set such a revolutionary process in motion is what he calls "society": a cultivated elite made up of small groups of dissenters, animated by profound ideals and aiming, through a kind of cultural contagion, at the not immediately political goal of transforming consciences through words and example. "Today"—wrote Caffi—"the multiplication of groups of friends sharing the same anxieties and united by respect for the same values could have more importance than almost any propaganda machine. Such groups would not need compulsory rules nor orthodox ideologies. They would not rely on collective action, but rather on individual initiative and the solidarity that can exist among friends who know each other well and among whom no one pursues goals or personal power". Caffi had in mind the strength of the early Christians, lacking a "well-defined episcopal hierarchy", but capable of conquering entire peoples; and he had in mind the "the cenacles of libertines and encyclopedists" of the 18th century who were able to carry out "an irresistible propaganda, establishing contacts among free spirits from one end of Europe to the other". In short, he had in mind groups driven by the goal of transforming "ways of thinking and customs rather than things, society rather than institutions" and so able to bring "a real change into the world".[367]

What's Left?

As we have seen, Caffi's ideas deeply influenced Macdonald, as is shown by many of the arguments he advances in *The Root is Man*.[368] One might

---

367 A. Caffi, *Critique of Violence*, pp. 87–88.

368 On this, I must refer to A. Castelli, "Le nuove strade della politica", in H. Arendt, A. Caffi, P. Goodman, D. Macdonald, *politics e il nuovo socialismo*, Genova-Milano, Marietti, 2012, pp. 9–86.

even argue, however, that—albeit in an indirect and circuitous way—Caffi's perspective has gone well beyond the pages written by Macdonald and by a few of his European disciples. In his seminal study of the *politics* circle, Gregory Sumner presents the reflections of Caffi, Macdonald, and other contributors to the journal as anticipating a tendency that would gain wide acceptance between the 1950s and the 1970s. Sumner, in this connection, cites Martin Luther King Jr. and the American civil rights movement; Václav Havel[369], the anti-Soviet dissident; and the Hungarian anti-Soviet writer György Konrád.[370] Men and movements that sought—often with success—to bring about social and political change through a strategy of struggle grounded in the revolution of consciences and in opposition carried out in the name of ethical principles.[371]

Today, then, we know that those ideas, which Caffi had already arrived at in the 1930s, in the midst of the anti-fascist struggle, must be taken seriously. We know that many nonviolent struggles aimed at "transforming ways of thinking" before transforming things themselves achieved success in the second half of the twentieth century. And, conversely, we know that many military victories of the oppressed, after seizing political power, have turned dreams of freedom into authoritarian nightmares, as millions of inhabitants of Indochina, Latin America, and Africa can testify. From such experiences we should certainly not draw the conclusion that political violence is always inappropriate, nor that the kind of struggle Caffi proposes is a one-size-fits-all solution: history and politics are highly complex realms, and general laws can never be formulated. Rather, those experiences prompt us to recognize that Caffi had excellent reasons for warning us against believing that violence is conducive to building a more civil society, and for insisting that a liberation struggle worthy of the name would do well to 'subordinate politics to certain broader spiritual values' and to channel revolutionary energies toward immediately creative aims. In short, they lead us to recognize that Caffi was not wrong in arguing that the most effective

---

369 (Editorial Footnote): Václav Havel (1936–2011), dissident under Communism, subsequently President of Czechoslovakia 1989–1992, the President of the Czech Republic 1993–2003.

370 (Editorial Footnote): György Konrád (1933–2019), Hungarian dissident author under Communism.

371 G.D. Sumner, *Dwight Macdonald,* pp. 175–178.

response to oppression—what can truly eliminate it—often consists in radically rejecting the violent world of the oppressor and the use of his oppressive means, and in trying to cultivate within oneself the kind of coexistence one wishes to bring about.

Alberto Castelli

Bibliography

1. Works by Andrea Caffi in Chronological Order:

"The Automatization of European People" (by "European"), *politics*, No. 10, November 1945.

"Towards a Socialist Program" (by "European"), *politics*, No. 12, December 1945.

"Is Revolutionary War a Contradiction in Terms? A Letter from "European", *politics*, No. 27, April 1946.

"Notes on Mass Culture" (by "European"), *politics,* No. 33, November 1946.

"Violence and Sociability" (by "European"), *politics,* No. 36, January 1947.

"The French Condition" (by "European"), *politics,* No. 38, July/August 1947.

"On Mythology", *possibilities*, No. 1, Winter 1947/48.

"A Glance at Marx's Horizons", *Instead,* probably No. 1, early 1948.

"Machine and Myth", *Instead,* No. 3, possibly March 1948.

"The Myth and Politics" (with Nicola Chiaromonte), *Instead,* probably No. 7, late 1948/early 1949.

"In Today's Newspaper", *Instead,* probably No. 7, late 1948/early 1949.

"Mass Politics and the Pax Americana", in Dwight Macdonald, *The Root is Man,* Alhambra (CA), The Cunningham Press, 1953, pp. 62-63.

Andrea Caffi, *A Critique of Violence*, Indianapolis, Bobbs-Merrill, 1970.

Andrea Caffi, *Scritti politici,* Firenze, La Nuova Italia, 1970.

Andrea Caffi, "Lettera a Carlo Rosselli", in *Storia in Lombardia*, XVI, No. 2, 1996.

Andrea Caffi, *La dottrina fascista. O il fascismo nella storia superiore del pensiero,* (ed. Alberto Castelli), Milan, Biblion, 2022.

Other Authors.

Lionel Abel, "Innocence and the Intellectual", *The New Republic*, 24 March 1986.

Lionel Abel, *The Intellectual Follies*, New York, W W Norton and Co, 1984.

Lionel Abel, "What is Society? The Ideas of Andrea Caffi", *Commentary*, Vol. 50, No. 3, September 1970.

Valerio Angeletti, Amanda Swain, "The *Lampadophorous*: Paolo Milano, Nicola Chiaromonte and the politics of Friendship", *Forum Italicum*, Vol. 59, 1, 2025.

Hannah Arendt, Andrea Caffi, Paul Goodman, Dwight Macdonald, (ed. A.Castelli), *politics e il nuovo socialismo*, Genova-Milano, Marietti, 2012.

Randolph Bourne, *War and Intellectuals. Collected Essays 1915-1919*, (ed. C. Resek), New York, Harper and Row, 1964 (Second Edition Indianapolis, Hackett Publishing Company), 1999.

Marco Bresciani, "Andrea Caffi's Intellectual Itinerary: A Long-Standing Loyalty to Herzen in the Twentieth Century", *Russica Romana*, XV, 2008.

Mario Bresciani, (ed.), *«Cosa Sperare?» Il carteggio tra Andrea Caffi e Nicola Chiaromonte: un dialogo sulla rivoluzione (1932-1955)*, Napoli, Edizioni Scientifiche Italiane, 2012.

Marco Bresciani, *La rivoluzione perduta, Andrea Caffi nell'Europa del Novecento*, Bologna, il Mulino, 2009.

Marco Bresciani, *Learning from History,* London, Verso, 2024.

Marco Bresciani, "Socialism, Fascism and Anti-Totalitarianism", *History of European Ideas*, Vol. 40, No. 7, 2014.

Alberto Castelli, *The Peace Discourse in Europe*, London, Routledge, 2019.

Nicola Chiaromonte, *The Worm of Consciousness*, New York, Harcourt Brace Jovanovitch, 1977.

Joseph Robert Conlin (ed.), *The American Radical Press. 1880–1960*, Westport – London, Greenwood press, 1974, Vol. I.

Antonio Donno, *Dal New Deal alla Guerra fredda. Aspetti del radicalismo statunitense negli anni '40*, Firenze, Sansoni, 1983.

T.S. Eliot, *Notes Towards the Definition of Culture*, London, Faber, 1962.

"Gallicus", "The Liberals' "Indispensable Man": Hitler", *politics*, No. 12, January 1945.

Ann Eden Gibson, *Issues in Abstract Expressionism: The Artist Run Periodicals*, Ann Arbor, UMI Research Press, 1990.

Natalia Ginzburg, *Family Lexicon*, London, Daunt Books, 2018.

Georges Gurvitch, "Mass, Community, Communion", *The Journal of Philosophy*, Vol. 38, No. 18, 1941.

Georg G. Iggers (translation and introduction), *The Doctrine of Saint-Simon: An Exposition. First Year 1828–1829.* Boston, Beacon Press, 1958.

Arthur Koestler, *Bricks to Babel,* New York, Random House, 1980.

Marion Labeÿ, "Andrea Caffi et la Révolution Bolchevique, Une crise personelle au «crepuscule de la civilization europeénne» (1917-1923)", *Cahiers Jaurès*, Vol. 1, No. 239-240, 2021..

Gianpiero Landi (ed.) *Andrea Caffi un socialista libertario*, Pisa, Biblioteca Franco Serantini,1996.

Melvin J. Lasky, "The Breadline and the Movies", *politics*, No. 1, February 1944.

Dwight Macdonald, "A Theory of Popular Culture", *politics*, No. 1, February 1944.

Dwight Macdonald, *The Root is Man,* Alhambra (CA), The Cunningham Press, 1953.

Dwight Macdonald, *The Root is Man,* Brooklyn, Autonomedia, 1995.

Dwight Macdonald, "Why "POLITICS"?", *politics,* No. 1, February 1944.

Clara Malraux, *Et pourtant j'étais libre,* Paris, Grasset, 1979.

Peter Meyer, "Mr. Joseph Stalin's Revolution in Economic Science", *politics,* No. 5, June 1944.

Harold Orlansky, "The Journey Home", by Mass Observation, (Book Review), *politics,* No. 11, December 1944.

Stanislao G. Pugliese, *Carlo Rosselli, Socialist Heretic and Antifascist exile,* Cambridge (Mass), Harvard University Press, 1999.

Jed Rasula, *Acrobatic Modernism from the Avant-Garde to Prehistory,* Oxford, Oxford University Press, 2020.

Jean-Paul Sartre, *Being and Nothingness,* London, Methuen & Co., 1957.

Giles Scott-Smith, Charlotte Lerg (eds.), *Campaigning Culture and the Global Cold War: The Journals of the Congress for Cultural Freedom,* London, Palgrave MacMillan, 2017.

Victor Serge, *Memoirs of a Revolutionary, 1901–1941 ,* New York, New York Review of Books Classics, 2012.

Frances Stonor Saunders, *Who Paid the Piper? The CIA and the Cultural Cold War,* London, Granta, 2000.

Gregory Sumner, *Dwight Macdonald and the politics Circle,* Ithaca, Cornell University Press, 1996.

Amanda Swain, "'One of the last secret maestros': Nicola Chiaromonte between Europe and America", *Journal of Modern Italian Studies*, Vol. 29, No. 2, 2024.

Amanda Swain, "Utopia in New York: Nicola Chiaromonte and the New York Intellectuals' "Superstition of Science"", *Modern Intellectual History*, Vol. 21, 2024.

W. P. Taylor, "So What? Some Reactions to Current Criticisms of Russia", *politics*, No. 11, December 1944.

Mike Tyldesley, *Liberate and Federate*, Sparnäs, Irene Publishing, 2024.

Franco Venturi, *Roots of Revolution*, London, Phoenix Press, 2001.

Laurence Veysey, *The Communal Experience: Anarchist and Mystical Counter-Cultures in America*, New York, Harper and Row, 1973.

Susan Weissman, *Victor Serge: The Course is Set on Hope*, London, Verso, 2001.

Hugh Wilford, *The New York Intellectuals. From Vanguard to Institution*, Manchester, Manchester University Press, 1995.

James D Wilkinson, *The Intellectual Resistance in Europe*, Cambridge (Mass), Harvard University Press, 1981.

Michael Wreszin, *A Rebel in Defence of Tradition: The Life and politics of Dwight Macdonald*, New York, Basic Books, 1994.

Index

About the Contributors

Mike Tyldesley was a lecturer in Politics at Manchester Metropolitan University for more than a quarter of a century. Now retired, he has produced books and articles, including studies on Socialists, Pacifists and the counterculture. His most recent book was *Liberate and Federate* (2024).

Alberto Castelli teaches History of Political Thought at the University of Insubria, Italy. His research focuses on pacifist and libertarian theories in the twentieth century. He edited the new Italian edition of *Critique of Violence* (2017) by Andrea Caffi and the publication of Andrea Caffi's manuscript *La dottrina fascista* (2022).

www.ingramcontent.com/pod-product-compliance
Lightning Source LLC
Chambersburg PA
CBHW030934060726
47591CB00005B/1788